Praise for the Dating Goddess

The Adventures in Delicious Dating After 40 series of books is based on the blog Adventures in Delicious Dating After 40 at www.DatingGoddess.com. Here are comments from readers.

💜 "ISO King Charming is a uniquely intelligent, witty, useful, and candid discussion of how real single women in the actual world handle authentic relationships. The Dating Goddess speaks with humor and authority, as one mature woman to another, and offers advice as well as perspective in every breezy, lively paragraph."

—Gina Barreca, Ph.D., bestselling author, *It's Not That I'm Bitter: How I Learned To Stop Worrying About Visible Panty Lines and Conquered the World*

💜 "At last, a dating writer who addresses requirements. You are SO right on! I'm thrilled to have found you!" —Rachel Sarah, author, *Single Mom Seeking*

"Adventures in Delicious Dating After 40 is a wonderful composite of both the mechanics of post-40 online dating and what the practice of honoring one's self actually looks like. How marvelous your writing is to read. I spent about 2 hours reading and was riveted the whole time."
—Maggie Hanna

"Powerfully heartfelt and honest writing. You are inspiring." —Kare Anderson, Emmy Award winning writer

"I just love your writing. It is very fresh and gives the reader something to think about." —Kelly Lantz, President & Manager, 55-Alive.com

"Dating Goddess, you are like a, a, a, well, a goddess to me. You've helped guide me successfully through my re-entry into the dating world after 14 years. I'm an eager student and fast study, and do get myself into situations that others don't know how to deal with — such as 3 dates in one day -— so thankfully you are there! You're the greatest, thanks for all you do for us!" —Jae G.

"I find your point of view much more interesting than other dating writers. Thanks for always reminding me to enjoy dating life no matter what it throws at you." —Sandy

"I love Adventures in Delicious Dating After 40. I really do like your honest and authentic voice — it's refreshing." —Wendy S.

Check Him Out *Before* Going Out

Avoiding Dud Dates

by **Dating Goddess**

In Search of King Charming: Who Do I Want to Share My Throne?

Second Edition

Cover design by Dave Innis, www.innisanimation.com

Book design by JustYourType.biz

Printed in the United States of America.

ISBN   Print: 978-1-930039-35-3

eBook: 978-1-930039-1-31

How to order:

The *Adventures in Delicious Daing After 40* books may be ordered directly from www.DatingGoddess.com.

Quantity discounts are also available. Visit us online for updates and additional articles.

The Adventures in Delicious Dating After 40 books are dedicated to my ex-husband since he unexpectedly released me to explore the untethered life of a single woman. I then had the freedom for the experiences, lessons and insights shared in these pages.

Books by Dating Goddess

Contents

x

Introduction

This book is designed for anyone who is interested in stories, advice, and lessons from the midlife dating front. If you are over 40 and haven't dated in a while — or even if you have — you'll learn ways to approach dating with zeal, optimism, and hope. Even if you've had more than your share of negative experiences, I'll share how to glean lessons from those adventures, rather than just declaring that "all men are jerks" or "men are just looking for sex."

While most of the perspective is from a woman to women, men's comments, experiences, and lessons have been integrated as appropriate.

This book began as daily entries into my blog, Adventures in Delicious Dating After 40, which has been featured in the *Wall Street Journal* as well as on radio and TV. I wrote about my epiphanies from my and my friends' dating life. The best postings were culled to make this and subsequent books.

This book focuses on helping you better define what you want in your next mate, beyond tall, dark and handsome! In midlife you want something different than what you wanted when you were younger. This book will help you look at what you want now.

xi

This book consists of three types of perspectives:

Lessons: These are specific experiences I thought would be useful to you. A few lines from my experience illustrate the points.

Insights: These usually start with an experience I've encountered, then the insights that experience spawned. It is usually comprised of around half story and half insight.

Stories: These are examples of situations I've experienced — or was currently experiencing when I wrote that piece — that I thought would be entertaining. Or I thought the story would help you see what kind of things happen in the midlife dating world so you'd know what has happened to others.

Because these writings were real time, as they occured, they are often set in the present tense. But they are not chronological. So a reference to "my current beau" may now be many sweethearts ago. I hope this isn't confusing.

I'd love ot hear your stories and questions. Please email them to me at Goddess@DatingGoddess.com. They may make it into the blog or my next book!

Who is the Dating Goddess?

I am a middle-aged, white, professional woman. My husband of nearly 20 years left me in April 2003 when I was 47, 11 days shy of 48. After giving my heart time to heal from the surprise divorce sprung by the man I thought was my soulmate, I started dating 18 months later. Generally, I have had a great time meeting interesting men, some of whom became romantic beaus, some became treasured friends, and some I never heard from again.

> *I am not a well-preserved, gorgeous, marathon-running middle-aged women*

In the beginning, I had dates with single male colleagues, but I quickly found Internet dating was the way to explore the most "inventory" and qualify men who I thought might be a good match.

I am not one of those well-preserved, gorgeous,

marathon-running middle-aged women. I have been told I am attractive, but I am overweight and not a gym rat. So while I am active, I do not match the description 90% of men's profiles say they want: slender, athletic, toned, fit. I have some wrinkles — what one sweet suitor mistakenly called dimples. I have what Bridget Jones called "wobbly bits," as most non-surgically enhanced middle-aged women do. My genes — and a lifetime addiction to chocolate — have made their mark. Yet I've met and dated some wonderful men, so even if you're not a lingerie model, you can find guys who will think you're attractive, perhaps even hot!

In my professional life, I am a bestselling author of workplace effectiveness books, professional speaker and management consultant. I've appeared on Oprah, 60 Minutes, and National Public Radio and in the *Wall Street Journal* and *USA Today*.

This book is intended to not only be useful to others and cathartic for me, but is also the genesis of a new topic for fun, thought-provoking speeches. I'm calling myself a dating philosopher and giving date-a-vational speeches! Let me know if you know a group who would like an entertaining after-lunch speech on how lessons learned from dating have implications in business and personal relationships and well as life philosophies.

How did I come by the Dating Goddess moniker? After a few months of dating dozens of men — one week yielded 7 dates with 6 guys in 5 days — my friends dubbed me this name. I liked it, so it stuck.

I'm purposefully not sharing my picture as I don't want you to think either, "How did she get any dates at all?" or the opposite, "Of course she found it easy to get 112 men to ask her out." I am not hideous (usually) nor am I stunning (without professional hair, makeup and Photoshop!). Some men find me attractive, some don't.

I continue to search for my "one," but I have learned a lot along the way, and my single and not-single friends have loudly encouraged me to share my experiences and lessons in the hopes of helping others navigate the adventure of dating with more success. And to have a delicious time doing it!

Make sure to download your free eBook Attract Your Next Great Mate: Dating Advice From Top Relationship Experts *at www. DatingGoddess.com/freebie*

Building your Franken-boyfriend

I've fantasized about putting together my perfect man — my Franken-boyfriend. After dating a lot of men, I've grown very fond of different parts of many. I'd like to build my perfect man with the beautiful green eyes of one, the height of another, one's sense of humor, another's deep, resonant voice, the kindness and sensitivity of one, the dancing skills of another, one's superior intelligence, the kisses of another, the attentiveness of one, the adventurousness of another, one's business acumen, the caresses of another, one's playfulness, another's sense of style.

> *I've grown very fond of different parts of many man*

If you were to put together your Franken-boyfriend, what characteristics would you pull from your male pals or fantasy dates?

It's important to identify what's important to you, but to realize that outside the movies, one man who contains all those attributes probably doesn't exist. So be clear on what is most important to you.

One way to become clear is to notice what you like and don't like about your dates. Keep a list of each. You'll discover that something you thought you wanted gets on your nerves if overdone. I like whomever I'm dating to call and touch base each day. However, I realized there was a limit to this when one boyfriend called 5-6 times a day to tell me what he was doing. I like affection, but one guy's kissing me every 10 minutes was too much.

So notice what you want in your Franken-boyfriend and be prepared that you may fall for someone who doesn't have some characteristics you thought were very important!

What's your "perfect boyfriend's" job description?

It has been said that first dates are like job interviews, with both sides interviewing for the other's position of "sweetheart/lover/mate."

While most daters have made an effort to list characteristics of their perfect mate (the candidate's qualifications), they don't usually list their own expectations (the actual job description).

I dated a guy who interviews and hires people for a living, I decided to put our relationship in his language — a job description. When I told him I wanted to play a game with him, he said fine. I said, "Mr. X, I understand there is an opening for Mr. X's girlfriend. What are the candidate's requirements and the job description?"

He laughed. *"Well, she needs to be smart, beautiful on the inside, and fun."*

"Hmm. What about beautiful on the outside? You have to be attracted to her, right?"

"Yes. But if she's beautiful on the inside, that will come through."

"No requirements for body shape or height? Most men have some preferences here."

"I'm a leg man. I like good legs."

"'Good legs' has different definitions for different people. Are you thinking the legs of Cameron Diaz, Beyonce, or Queen Latifah?"

"Beyonce," he said firmly. "Cameron Diaz' legs are too skinny."

"What about touch? Do you like touch?"

"There's touch and then there's Touch. The latter needs to be behind closed doors."

And on we went. I found it helpful to clarify what he meant when he used nebulous words. Then I shared what I was looking for in my guy's job description. But I realized that I, like most people, had clearly written the candidate's characteristics (tall, smart, funny, nice

> *I clarified what he meant when he used nebulous words*

looking, active, chivalrous, accomplished), but I had overlooked the true job description. I have flushed out what I've begun to notice that I like and want. Here it is.

Job description of the Goddess's perfect boyfriend

Seeking self-starting, action-oriented, smart, fun, playful, tall (6'0"+), physically active man, age 48-62, wanted for long-term relationship with tall, affectionate, fun, smart, playful, accomplished, thoughtful, feisty, positive Goddess. The top candidate will receive benefits far beyond what most others offer and these will be fully disclosed to the top qualified candidates. They include lots of kissing, caressing, cuddling and more, passion, understanding, respect, kindness, fun activities, home-cooked meals, laughter, support of your endeavors, positive attitude and feedback.

The job entails:

- Treating the Goddess like someone loved and cherished. This includes, but is not limited to, talking every day, being chivalrous (opening doors, etc.), romance (sweet talk, compliments, planning outings, flowers, surprises).

- Working out any disagreements, rather than clamming up or disappearing.

- Being loyal and not seeking other women.

- Being a passionate and giving lover who also openly receives. Great kissing required.

- Giving grace if the Goddess does something he initially interprets as negative.

- Sharing feelings about life and our relationship on a regular basis.

- Working to continually improve himself and his environment.

- Being financially mature and responsible.

- Living his life with personal integrity, including but not limited to, doing what he says he will, calling when he promises, doing what's right, not necessarily what's easy.

- Having the courage to bring up difficult topics, and engaging maturely when the Goddess does the same.

- Consciously taking care of his body so he is healthy and active.

- Laughing at the Goddess's attempts to be funny.

- Socializing willingly and pleasantly in groups or with friends, both his and hers.

- Planning outings like dancing, foreign films, dinners out, theater, parties, concerts, and other activities both enjoy. Initiating plans for events he thinks the Goddess would like, proposing them, and then arranging for the tickets, etc.

- Participating in physical activities together (biking, hiking, walking, dancing) or alone (working out, running, golf, other sports). Regular physical activity a must.

At their request, I've gone over these requirements with a few prospective suitors before we meet and discussed each one to see which ones they were with and which ones needed negotiation.

Start writing your boyfriend's job description now.

A man to go with
your wardrobe

Our lifestyle is often reflected by the clothing we're most comfortable wearing, which often represents the activities we enjoy. Most of us have a range of clothing from sweats to business attire to formal apparel.

We know how important first impressions are. While successful people would never show up for a job interview inappropriately dressed, I've been surprised how many men show up for a first date giving apparently no thought to how they want to be perceived.

> *I'm surprised when men give no thought to how they want to be perceived.*

When I first started dating, I realized I didn't have dateware — casual clothing in which I felt attractive and current. I had abundant business clothes, very casual duds and some formal attire. Shopping for dateware helped me reinvent how I wanted to represent myself on dates.

Most of my dates wear basic collared shirts and Dockers or jeans to coffee or a casual dinner. Occasionally a guy will wear a sports jacket. But rarely do they wear clothes that stand out as classy.

So imagine my delight when I started dating a man who prides himself on dressing nicely. I called him my "GQ" guy — he was not pretentious, but wore ironed silk shirts with gabardine slacks to the movies and dinner. Even with jeans, he wore a crisp golf shirt. I enjoyed going out with him for many reasons, one of which is that I could wear my nicer garb and not feel overdressed.

I think dressing nicely not only shows respect for yourself, but for the other person. Just as most of us wouldn't go to church in shorts and a t-shirt out of respect. Not that a guy needs to wear silk shirts for a day at the beach or a hike, but I appreciate it when my date goes to some effort when going out. While a guy's dress isn't a deal breaker for me, when he dresses well, it's icing on the cake.

How do you feel about how your date dresses?

Are you drawn to "Oscar" or "Felix"?

D o you like guys who are more Oscar-like or more like Felix? Recently, I got to test for myself.

For 7 weeks I dated a guy who was a lot like Jack Klugman's character Oscar Madison in "The Odd Couple." While a very sweet, smart, affectionate, attentive guy, he always looked rumpled. He was even disheveled naked! I began to doubt the man owned an iron — if he did he either had no idea where it was or no clue how to use it.

When I visited his house, it was decorated in "early student" — torn couch, dust everywhere, crumbs on the floor so I didn't dare go barefoot. The cobwebs were so thick in every corner they looked like ropes. I had to ask him to wipe the TV screen before watching a DVD because I couldn't see the picture. I didn't like to eat or drink there because the dishes looked like they hadn't been washed. His front yard was so weed covered, I began to pull some while we had wine on his leaf-littered porch. The back yard was so overgrown, he'd received nuisance citations from the city two years in a row!

Needless to say, I didn't accept many invitations to visit him there.

Contrast that to a guy who was more like Tony Randall's character Felix Unger. Fastidious was his middle name. His car was spotless inside and out. His luxury penthouse apartment appeared to be straight out of *Architectural Digest*. His dining room was pre-set with china for six — even though he's never had a dinner party at this place.

He had three color-coordinated pot holders on the kitchen counter, meticulously spaced. His bathroom towels are hung with a bath towel, a contrasting hand towel over that, another contrasting towel arranged horizontally around the previous one. No one would ever use any of them like this! After using the chenille throw while watching TV, I folded it and placed it back in its place when done. I later noticed he'd refolded it!

He always looked crisp, something I admire. In the six times we went out, he always looked clean and pressed. If I didn't know better, I'd guess that he irons his briefs! Although thankfully, he doesn't apparently iron his jeans.

Which do you prefer? Or do you like a hybrid?

Which do I prefer? Felix wins hands down! While "anal-retentive" does come to mind, I'm much happier around someone who gives some attention to looking good and to living in a clean environment. I am aware, however, that meticulousness can translate into perfectionist and control freak.

In search of the elusive good kisser

"A man's kiss is his signature." — *Mae West*

I've been surprised by the lack of good kissers in my dating adventures. Granted, sometimes it takes a while to actually get a passionate kiss — if ever. It took six dates with one guy before I got a "real" kiss — something beyond a peck. On the other hand, several men have greeted me with a deep kiss as if we'd been dating for a while. The latter is not my preference. I like to get to know someone and be drawn to him before I want to explore further, if you know what I mean.

Two men have told me they are planning on kissing me upon meeting. This does take some of the anxiety out of "will he kiss me?" — sometimes it seems premature.

Several stopped me while we were walking to plant the first kiss. Another, charmingly leaned over when he arose mid-meal to go to the men's room, "I need a little kiss to tide me over while I'm away from you." It was cute and worked to get me to hang out with him more.

"Whoever named it 'necking' was a poor judge of anatomy." — *Groucho Marx*

I've noticed if a man says in his profile that he's a good kisser, he often is not. With only one exception everyone who said he was a good kisser actually wasn't.

So I'm surprised that men in middle age don't know how to kiss better. One man I dated for six months was too much too fast, no kissing foreplay. Another was so sloppy I needed a napkin afterward. I could go on and on. I've been tempted to dog-ear the kissing section in *Mars and Venus in the Bedroom* for some suitors and put it in a place I know they'll see it.

A friend pointed out that perhaps other women have liked how these guys kissed. Or maybe they've just never had feedback. How do you say to someone, "You aren't a good kisser"? That's like saying, "You aren't a good lover." I've tried modifying their behavior by giving them positive feedback on the parts I like: "I love it when you nibble on my lips," or "I love the anticipation of our kisses when you kiss my face first." Some learn. Others don't.

Once I tried bringing it up with a particularly unpleasing kisser. I said, "Let's play a game. You kiss me how you like to be kissed and I'll kiss you how I like to be kissed." Even with that, not a lot changed.

I must admit I've hung out with some gentleman callers longer than I should have if they were good kissers. It's an elusive — but I hope not dying — art.

Rocket Man

I've become fond of a man online who blows things up for a living. Tiny things. Miniatures. For the movies. And he's won an Oscar for his demolition efforts.

Isn't this nearly every man's childhood dream? To make a living destroying things? How fun!

He specializes in igniting things. He says he "paints with fire." He's set himself ablaze 51 times — on purpose! For films, of course. He even filled in for a flaming Arnold Schwarzenegger in one film. How am I supposed to light his fire when he's torched himself 51 times?

How am I supposed to light his fire when he's torched himself 51 times?

While sometimes his charges are detonated inside the object, other times he launches a projectile to explode the target. He uses rockets. So my pet name for him has become Rocket Man, which he likes.

If we hit it off, it will be good to know I can turn

to him if I need anything around the house blown up. Instead of "Honey, could you spray that ant hill in the back?" it would be "Honey, could you blow up that ant hill in the back?"

That little golden statue may be nice to have around the house. I can see dressing him up for each month's holidays — an Easter Bunny outfit, a Halloween costume, a Santa's hat. Maybe we'd give him a Barbie harem. Would he fit in the Malibu Barbie car? I don't think so.

Since his specialty is pyrotechnics, I'd expect fireworks with our first kiss. I wonder if he could arrange that without any building blowing up.

So far his personality seems to be far from explosive, however sparks fly via email and phone conversations. I wonder what makes a sweet, humble man like to blow things up. I'll find out soon enough.

And get this — his favorite drink is a Bomb-bay martini!

Let's hope he's not a dud, but instead da bomb

When you're clear on what you want, it appears

In the past few years I attended both the Toronto and San Jose Film Festivals. I loved screening yet-to-be-released films followed by live commentary from the writers, directors and stars. I delighted in the experience so much, I thought, "I'd like to be with someone in the movie business. It would be fun to hang out with people in the industry."

A few months later, enter Rocket Man, a man who works in Hollywood. In our first week's hours-long phone conversations and daily multiple emails, he invited me to Academy-members-only film viewings and — get this — the Academy Awards ceremony! Serendipity? Maybe. Maybe not.

You may be saying, "I'm clear on what I want! I want a loving, mature, romantic, fun-loving, financially sound, emotionally available guy who will treat me well. So why haven't I found him yet?" I understand your frustration.

Doug Hooper, an early mentor and author of *You Are What You Think*, said our wishes go to a giant shipping department in the sky. Sometimes the shipping clerk receives what seems is an incomplete order. The clerk needs to know how tall your guy should be. How old? How close to you should he be living? Should he want to have kids? Your "unit" can't be shipped until you fill in the missing info. But the clerk doesn't have a way to tell you the info is missing, so you become frustrated.

💜 Unfortunately, sometimes the orders get lost. You need to keep sending your order, but each time check for completeness. Add anything you notice is missing. I've written down my order. (See "What's your 'perfect boyfriend's' job description?" page 2.)

Our wishes go to a giant shipping department

💜 Sometimes the order is complete, but the "unit" is unavailable or still being completed to your specs. Maybe he's currently with someone else so you have to wait weeks or months for him to become available. Or maybe he's still bitter about his last relationship and if you were to meet him now, he wouldn't be emotionally available. The shipping department waits until he's ready to be shipped

to you. Or maybe it's you who's not quite ready, even though you think you are.

🖤 However, you also have to be willing to accept what the universe ships, if he's close to what you want. No one is 100% perfect. Even the Earth-bound shipping process sometimes causes some damage in transit. You wanted a guy with a full head of hair and your current guy is perfect except he's bald? So what! He has a little baggage left over from the last relationship? I bet you do, too. Sometimes the best "units" — like priceless antiques — have slight dents or scratches.

🖤 Should you accept partial shipments? A guy who's only 50% of what you want? In "Building your Franken-boyfriend" (page 1), I discuss how great it would be if you could combine the desired characteristics from several men into one. However, if he's only 50% of your order, I think you should put him back into inventory — release him as he may be 95% of what someone else wants.

So was Rocket Man "the one"? No. But he had a lot of the characteristics of the man I will be with long term. I think he was The Shipping Department's idea of seeing if I'd accept a partial shipment. I also believe if I hadn't sent in my order months ago, he wouldn't have shown up.

What's your idea of boyfriend responsibilities?

"Boyfriend responsibilities" are not the same as "marital duties," but the latter can be included in the former. The man I was dating and I were discussing boyfriend responsibilities.

He apologized for not being more cognizant of his boyfriend responsibilities. He knew my garage door opener needed a minor repair. While I was conducting an hour-long client call he took a nap, which was fine with me. In his email he said, "I'm very sorry about the garage door. I should have jumped right on it." I hadn't asked him to fix it, nor did he say he would, so I didn't have any expectations that it would be magically fixed while I was otherwise engaged.

I don't expect my beau to be my ad-hoc handyman, unless it's something in which I know he has expertise and doesn't mind doing. He said, "My fingers shudder and refuse to let me pick up a hammer. Power tools have a restraining order against me. Changing oil means changing cars. Is there such a thing as an 'un-handyman'?"

As a homeowner, the never-ending list of "honey do's" keeps expanding. Even when I was married, I always had a handyman to do all but minor repairs. It saved us a lot of tension and fighting from my nagging my ex to do what I considered simple things, but he thought were time-consuming trips down frustration lane — as well as multiple visits to Home Depot.

I appreciate it when my beau takes initiative to help around the house

I may occasionally ask my sweetie to help out with a quick job, especially if it's something simple that I can't do by myself. I do a lot on my own, but some tasks need two people. Others are better delegated to my handyman so I can focus on other things.

I really appreciate it when my beau takes initiative to do anything that helps around the house and would fall on my shoulders otherwise. Without my asking, he's already emptied the dishwasher, cooked me breakfast and dinner, washed the dishes, fixed a nearly clogged faucet, brought in the mail, helped me prepare some packages for mailing, took out the trash, brought in firewood, and other things that he saw needed to be done. Since this week was an especially frazzled one, I'm grateful for anything he did to pitch in. And I appreciated it even more when I didn't have to ask or point out the task. It feels more like a partnership rather than his being a guest in my home.

What's your take on boyfriend duties? When you've been seeing someone for a little while, do you have any expectations of what he will do for you around the house? Do you discuss these expectations and see if he has any desire to take on these "honey do's"? Or is there tension and conflict because of different expectations? And what about when you're at his house? Does he expect you to do tasks that are traditionally "women's work" — mending, cooking, cleaning, laundry? If so, how do you handle it if you don't want to do the task, or don't have the skills?

"I don't want a whipped boyfriend"

These words were uttered by my neighbor's 16-year-old daughter as we were discussing dating. The three of us were sharing the nice things men we dated had done for us when she blurted this out. I was surprised, as I didn't think any of the examples we shared would be considered signs of a man being whipped.

"What's your definition of 'whipped'?" I asked.

"A guy who won't make a decision on his own. Who always gives in to the girl. My sister's boyfriend is like that. I don't like it."

"I don't blame you."

"When a guy won't stand up to his girlfriend, he's whipped. I want a guy who has his own opinions and thinks for himself, not always looking to me."

"I agree with you. While compromise is important for both people, you have to start with you both having your own opinion. However, sometimes I find I don't have a strong preference, so I'm willing to acquiesce, and sometimes it's he who doesn't feel strongly so capitulates to my way."

She got me thinking about the difference between whipped, wussy, amiable, and compromising. Some feel these are all pretty close on the amicable to combative continuum. While I like to hang out with someone who's agreeable, if he doesn't make his preferences known or doesn't disagree about anything, then I feel I am railroading him. I can be the "team leader" and make decisions for both of us, but frankly it is a lot of work and I prefer to share the load.

> *Do you like men on the milk toast end of the spectrum or more dominant?*

Where do you like your man to be on the continuum? Do you like men more on the milk toast end of the spectrum or more toward dominant? Or where in between?

And where would you place yourself on this continuum? On the submissive end or the domineering end? Not in an S & M sort of way, but just in how you live your life. And maybe you're different in your personal life than in your professional life. It's important to know so you can find a match who compliments you.

I dated a man briefly who told me he wanted a woman who would surrender to him. He said, "I don't want her to be submissive, but to surrender." When I asked him to explain the difference, he said, "I want a woman who will do what I want no matter if she wants to or not." I said, "That sounds like submissive to me." He also said if we were with other people I was not ever to disagree with anything he said. I wondered if he could spell "control." Needless to say, that does not describe what I was looking for, so we soon parted ways.

Long-distance dating
pros and cons

Some people set no distance requirements on potential suitors. One Adventures in Delicious Dating After 40 reader shared she was romanced by a guy half way around the world for over two years! (They never met and he went poof one day.)

Other people have ridiculously short distance requirements. Some men list 10 miles as their dating radius in their dating profiles. Unless you live in New York City, I think it this is too small. An hour's drive seems reasonable to me.

Throughout my post-divorce dating, I was always clear I didn't want a long-distance relationship. Even thinking that, I've been entranced enough with four of the 112 men to explore dating them. With three of the four, I spent hours on the phone with them, often talking every day for up to several months before meeting. Two I never saw after one date, and one I saw 3 times before he went poof.

Then I found myself in a 600-mile relationship. Why? Because he is a great, loving, smart, romantic, thoughtful guy. The distance has its pros and cons. Here's what I've found so far:

Pros:

💜 Because you aren't seeing each other frequently, you appreciate each other more.

💜 You plan special activities for when you are together.

💜 You spend compressed time together, so can get close fast.

💜 You send each other love notes/emails to keep the passion alive. More so than if you were within a short driving distance.

💜 You plan special romantic gestures to show the person you care after the visit — notes tucked in luggage or left on the refrigerator, chocolate hidden under the covers.

💜 Hellos and goodbyes are particularly sweet.

💜 You build up anticipation of spending time with your special guy.

💜 If you have a busy life, you can consolidate your dating into a few days a week/month/quarter rather than allotting time each week.

💜 You have plenty of time to see friends, work out, and participate in hobbies in between sweetie visits, so you don't feel you're cutting out activities you like while developing a relationship.

Cons:

💜 Easier to misinterpret things over the phone and email when the body language and facial expression are missing.

💜 If one of you is exhausted, sick or has to unexpectedly work, your together time is compromised. The person doing the travel may resent spending time and money to visit but not having the other's full attention.

You plan special activities for when you are together.

💜 Travel costs.

💜 Because of the compressed time (spending 2-3 days together nearly 24/7), you can move faster than you might if you saw each other in short few-hour spurts.

💜 Waiting too long between visits can strain the bond.

💜 Built-up expectations create unreasonable fantasies. We all have warts, but when you don't see someone regularly, you imagine them as perfect.

When the warts show up it's shocking.

♥ Resentments can fester if a special effort isn't made to talk about them.

♥ Might be tempting to see others.

On one hand, long-distance dating takes more effort. In addition to traveling to see one another, you need to take special effort to keep in touch on more than a superficial level in between. However, some relationships thrive on having a little time and space between the pair. I think it is easier if you have an already established relationship where circumstances require you to be apart for a few months or year. When developing a relationship, however, you both have to be clear the effort is worth it.

If you've long-distance dated, what have you found are the pros and cons?

Do you want an "E-Ticket" guy?

f you visited Disneyland or Disney World before 1982, you remember what an "E-Ticket" was. If you don't, it refers to the entrance tickets for the park's most thrilling or interesting rides, like the Matterhorn bobsled, and other state-of-the-art activities. If you were a normal kid, you loved the E-Ticket rides. As a 10-year-old, I remember my 15-year-old brother trying to snooker me out of my E-Tickets in exchange for his A-Tickets, which were for the sedate rides. But I didn't fall for it!

You try different categories of "rides" (dates)

Now in dating, I find guys falling into categories paralleling the ticket letters. An "A-Ticket" guy is nice, safe, and perhaps a bit boring. An "E-Ticket" guy is exciting, thrilling, and maybe a tad on the wild side.

The beauty of dating is you get to decide what kind of ticket you want. At Disneyland, you could buy a book of mixed ticket levels. In dating, that's what dating around is for. You try different categories of "rides" (dates) to see what you like. Maybe you decide you like mostly C- or D-Ticket type of dates (let's say that's dinner and listening to a band at a club). You then look for guys who like to do mostly those kinds of activities.

But what if you're an E-ticket gal and like on-the-edge recreation? Let's say that's rock climbing, parachute jumping, and motorcycle riding. If you find an E-ticket guy, you're in heaven. You know to steer clear of the A-Ticket guys who mostly like to read, play chess and watch TV.

My own preference is for a mixed-ticket guy. I like some E-Ticket activities, although my definition of E-Ticket doesn't include the ones listed above. I like exciting things (I've walked across a 12-foot bed of hot coals, climbed a 25-foot tall pole and leaped off, and swum with stingrays). But I like a cross-section of activities, sometimes including A-Ticket ones like reading, watching TV, and napping.

What's your preference? Have you discovered your optimal guy's ticket level? Or do you like a mix?

Do you think you'll change his mind?

Recently, I ran into a high-school buddy — someone I hadn't seen in over 30 years. He stopped me at our neighborhood's dance party, to which the whole city is invited. Out of 10,000 people, he picked me out of the crowd. I guess I haven't changed a great deal since high school!

Catching up, he shared with me the story of his post-divorce relationship. While dating a woman for 3 years, he insists he always told her he wasn't interested in marriage. However, near their third-year anniversary, she dragged him to her therapist and unbeknownst to him, demanded he tell her and the therapist why he wouldn't marry her.

His response was he never intended to marry her and he'd told her that all along. If this is true, apparently she expected she would be able to change his mind, then became disappointed and angry when he didn't. Her therapist told her she was delusional and they broke up within the month.

I, too, have been caught in the trap of thinking I could get a man to change his mind. When I first met my ex, he stated that he wasn't looking for a relationship. He was raising his son alone, had a full-time job, and freelanced on the side. He didn't have time for a relationship. I guess he just wanted occasional booty calls. But I, never having been married, wanted a relationship.

I acted like this "no relationship" deal was fine

In fact, I wanted a husband. I acted like this "no relationship" deal was fine, all the while whittling down his resistance until we were engaged eight months later and married eighteen months after that.

I had another goal in mind, one which he also stated he didn't share. I wanted children. Since he already had a child, and is 14 years older than me, he said he wasn't interested in more. However, I saw how much he loved and doted on his son, and I was sure he would want me to have the same experience. He loved kids, so I thought I could convince him otherwise, as I'd done with changing his mind about wanting a relationship.

I was wrong.

In retrospect, I should have believed him about not wanting a relationship, too. While he worked on making our marriage hum, I never felt he was as committed as I was. No fault to him, really. I should have believed him and looked for a man who was interested in building a family together.

I've been on the receiving end of someone wanting me to change my mind. When a logn-distance beau asked if I wanted to move to his city — 600 miles away — I said no. I'd told him all along I had no pull to his city. When the we broke up, he threw this in my face, saying that it showed how selfish I was. Had I been more committed to the relationship, which I wasn't after only 3 months, I would have at least seriously considered a move. But I was not willing to pretend I'd move to his city while we were just in dating mode. If it progressed to a committed relationship, we would have explored where we both wanted to live and found a mutually-agreeable location. His expecting me to change my mind was ignoring my clearly stated perspective.

If a man states something clearly to you — like he doesn't want to be in a relationship or get married again — believe him. Yes, he may change his mind, but don't proceed expecting that to happen. You'll be disappointed and angry, and may feel you wasted your time with him. But if he told you early on his point of view and you ignored it, don't blame him.

Are you dating the same guy in different bodies?

ou may be familiar with the poem "There's a Hole in My Sidewalk: Autobiography in Five Short Chapters" by Portia Nelson. In the poem, Ms. Nelson concisely illustrates how we make choices, have an unpleasant experience, and blame others. Then we learn from our experiences, take responsibility for our choices, and ultimately make different ones. I think it applies not only to life in general, but to dating.

How is this like dating? Have you found that sometimes you're attracted to the same kind of guy, perhaps with behaviors similar to your ex? Then you're upset that the guys treat you like your ex treated you. And you blame them. The cycle continues. Until you wake up to your part in the repetition.

You have probably heard the oft-quoted line, "The definition of insanity is doing the same thing over and over and expecting different results*." It's that way with dating. We're drawn to certain characteristics in a man that seem familiar to us, no matter how dysfunctional.

At least we are if we are unaware of how and why we keep dating the same guy in a different body over and over again. He's attractive to us because he feels so comfortable. In fact, sometimes we may actually utter, "It felt like we'd known each other a long time." Or, "It just felt right."

If we aren't conscious, we'll keep walking down the same sidewalk and falling in the same hole (dating the same kind of guy who treats us the same way our ex did). And we blame the guys for being losers, jerks, players, cads. It's not our fault!

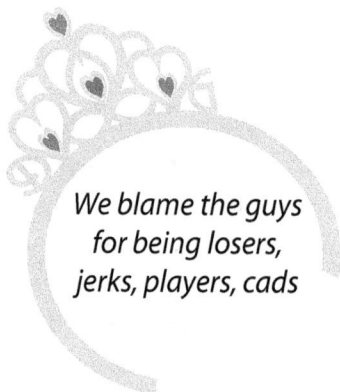

> *We blame the guys for being losers, jerks, players, cads*

Until one day, we get frustrated having fallen in the same hole once again! We know this time it is our fault, but it doesn't help lessen the pain. So we keep dating. Drat — once again we find ourself in the same hole (with another guy who is self-absorbed, inconsiderate, emotionally unavailable, or worse). This time we know it is our fault. We look inside, self-reflecting, asking why we keep choosing to go out with guys who have similar patterns. Maybe we get some counseling to clear it up. Our eyes are opened.

We continue to date. Now, however, we've become more discerning. We begin to ask key questions before we even meet the potential date. We know how to spot the patterns that have kept us stuck in bad relationships in the past. We say "no" more often to those who seem so familiar, but we know by what they say on the phone they would not be right for the new us.

And finally, we meet a guy who has none (or very few) of the familiar faults. He treats us respectfully, kindly, lovingly, appreciatively. We love being with him and he with us. We have walked down a new street.

* This is attributed to various people, including Benjamin Franklin and Albert Einstein.

Hot sex and laughter

"The only reason to give another adult your house key is for laughter and hot sex." —Regina Barreca, Ph.D.

Dr. Barreca said this in a keynote speech I heard her deliver. I thought it was priceless, as is she. She is an amazing, hilarious, intelligent, insightful, fabulous author and speaker. Her books include *They Used to Call Me Snow White...But I Drifted*, *Too Much of a Good Thing Is Wonderful*, and *I'm With Stupid*.

Gina, as I learned to call her during a half-hour one-on-one the night before her speech, has a unique perspective on the differences in the sexes.

Gina'ssays we want a partner mainly for amusement.

Her point of view offered in the quote above shows she has boiled down our needs to be partnered to the basics: entertainment. Of course, "hot sex" could also imply procreation. But after that part of life has passed, it is indeed just entertainment — which doesn't mean it isn't great entertainment.

43

We can wax philosophical that our desire to share our lives with a romantic interest is to increase our satisfaction, overcome loneliness, acquire an activity partner, learn to love deeply, and create synergy. However, you can create these things largely with friends, so why look for someone to commit yourself to, especially in midlife when procreation is not an issue? Gina's quote says we want a partner mainly for amusement.

In all fairness, I didn't talk to her afterward so see if she felt there was more beyond this. I'll send her this posting and see if she has a comment. So since we don't know more about her ideas on this, we can right now only hear yours. What do you think about Gina's comment and how it relates to your desires?

"Are you man enough to be my man?"

This can be a common thought for powerful, successful, midlife dating women. It was expressed by Adventures in Delicious Dating After 40 reader Diamond in a question to me:

> I've been in business my whole life. A friend's mother shared this advice just prior to my running off to meet what I thought was the man of my dreams in London. She gently said, in a loving mother's voice, "Do you mind if I give you a piece of advice about your man in London? Please don't treat him like a business!"

> I have a hard time switching from client mode to date mode. I treat my date as I do my clients"— I want to know up front, "What are your goals and objectives?" This is me, who are you? BAM! I'm sure I'm too direct for the first call. This doesn't evolve over time — I want to know now so I don't waste time.

OMG — I don't know how to date! The last guy went packing after our initial call. Run Forrest! Run!

I even took a painting class to "get my girl on," "open my heart," take off my pants!

Getting a massage, I asked my body worker for insights. She quipped, "I wish you could see your back as I am seeing it now." Where are the ceiling mirrors when you need them? "Your right side is highly defined and your left side is lower, softer and not as defined as the right. The right side represents your male side and the left your female side. You are spending too much time in the male energy area of your life."

I asked, "Is there a book I can buy to be more like a girl?" So male of me.

Later that night, I shared with the elders who had become my temporary grandmothers what trans-pired during my massage and they, too, laughed. One wise soul responded, "Dear, you do not need a book to be more like a girl. Simply go to your heart more and less from your head."

So, my questions:

How do you find a man more man than yourself?

Where are all the strong men that love strong women?

What does a strong woman do to leave the busi-ness side at home on a date?

How do you stay in a "skirt" when dating when all you do all day is wear "pants" at work?

How do you date when you have never dated because you have a belief that you only date someone if you are going to marry them?

How do you overcome the "I don't want to waste my time" disease?

Diamond (and other strong women):

This is such a good inquiry. I, too, have struggled with this and am not sure I have answers, but perhaps some insights that will help you find your own answers.

Many midlife women have created great lives

Many of us midlife women have created great lives through our focus, power and assertiveness. This is effective in the male culture of work, dominated with war and sports metaphors. We've learned how to dress powerfully, not provocatively, speak clearly and directly, stand with poise and confidence. It is so part of who we are that we have forgotten there is another more feminine side.

The truly powerful, I believe, have learned how to adapt to each situation and behave in ways that make them successful. A general is gentle around children or the infirm, yet speaks assuredly to the troops. A CEO knows that behavior in the boardroom is different than at the company picnic. So, too, we must relearn what it's like to allow our femininity to come out and still be powerful.

I am not saying you need to dummy down who you are. I'm saying that there are men who will love you for your power and will also love you when you allow your vulnerabilities to surface.

I started my business at 24. I felt to be taken seriously I needed to look and behave man-like. I only wore man-tailored clothing, had a short, no-nonsense hair cut, light makeup and carried an all-business briefcase. I continued to do this long after my credibility had been established and the severity began to hinder my effectiveness, as the people I wanted to connect with were intimidated. With the help of a few image consultant friends who saw my image was not eliciting the response I wanted, they helped outfit me in more feminine, yet still powerful attire. I consciously softened my behavior to be more approachable, softer, more welcoming. I can now shift more readily from business mode to date mode, with not only my dress but my demeanor.

My suggestion is to be conscious of the behaviors that aren't working in dating, and to choose new ones. How do you know which are more welcoming? Since there's not a book on it ☺ (at least not one we know about), my suggestion is to find women role models from whom to learn. They can be friends, colleagues, or even those in the media. Watch what they do and adapt it for yourself. In your example of drilling a potential suitor on the first encounter, think beforehand what questions you could ask that would be gentler, yet still elicit the information you desire.

Also, it helped me to read several of the *Mars/Venus* books to understand that men want to be needed, and feel good about being useful to a woman. It helped me not feel I had to insist on splitting the check, or reciprocate every kind action a date made. I choose to give to him in ways he would appreciate, even if it was a smile, a word of sincere thanks, or a hug. My feminist bent felt I had to match everything equally, tit for tat. I've learned I can be feminist and feminine at the same time.

It's the yin and the yang of relationships that make them work. If both of you are yang, why do you need the other? The secret, I believe is to be able to be yang when the other is in yin and vice versa. My ex was pretty yin. He embraced his feminine side, and while not effeminate, he was nurturing. When my yang started to diminish and I let my yin side out more, I believe that's when our disconnect began. He didn't know how to be more yang. I could have chosen to go back into predominately yang mode, but that was not satisfactory anymore.

Are you drawn to deep-voiced men?

Another useless study was recently released that announced, "Women favor men with deep voices." Robin Thicke and Michael Jackson, sorry!

It's well known that many women are attracted to men with deep, Barry White-like voices. Part of my ex's allure was his resonant, radio-announcer voice (he had a radio show for a few years). Another radio-news-anchor friend was a babe magnet — women fell for his voice. And one suitor melted me before we even met by wooing me on the phone with his baritone pitch.

We now have research on this from David Feinberg, assistant professor in the Department of Psychology, Neuroscience and Behaviour at McMaster University in Hamilton, Ontario. He and his colleagues recently published their findings in Biology Letters, concluding that "men with low-voice pitch have higher reproductive success and more children born to them." Their thesis is based on studying the Hadza tribe of Tanzania which is a hunter-gatherer culture — one of the last. Since they have no modern birth control it was easy to determine that the men who have lower-pitched voices have more children.

In previous studies, Feinberg found that women find men with deeper voices to be more attractive, judging them to be more dominant, older, healthier and more masculine sounding. There is some speculation that women equate deeper voices with more testosterone, thus assuming the man will be more aggressive hunting and be a good provider for her and her children.

So the researchers surmise a deep-voiced man is more appealing to his woman, thus she is willing to copulate more often, spawning more offspring. Since this study was done with only 49 men between the ages of 18 and 55, there may have been other factors not included. We don't know how many of the 49 men had the coveted lower-pitched voices, so let's say half, 25. What if a number of these men had more sex because they were nicer to their woman, brought her more food so she's happy with him, had sex with more women, choose younger, more fertile women, knew how to please her, etc. The researchers are placing a lot of emphasis on one characteristic.

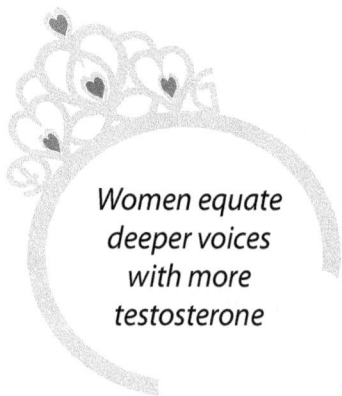

Women equate deeper voices with more testosterone

And if we believe in natural selection, the men with deep-voice genes would have passed these on to their offspring, and we would now be living in James-Earl-Jones- land. Nearly every man would have a resonant voice.

While I am casting dispersions on the summations of this study, intuitively I believe they are right — at least for midlife men and women. I'm sure younger women are more drawn to high-pitched voices than middle-aged women. While a falsetto can be entertaining from a singer, if a man's speaking voice is that high, most women won't find that enticing.

And what women's voices do men find appealing? Feinberg's previous studies showed men favor women with higher-pitch voices, saying they found these women more attractive, subordinate, feminine, healthier and younger sounding.

What have you noticed about a man's voice tone and your attraction to him? Do you find yourself drawn to men with lower voices, even if they aren't as attractive to you in other ways? And men, do you purposely lower your voice on the first call to communicate your masculinity?

Make sure to download your free eBook Attract Your Next Great Mate: Dating Advice From Top Relationship Experts *at www. DatingGoddess.com/freebie*

Prince Considerate

any women refer to their perfect man as Prince
Charming. We want someone who is likable and knows
what to say to get along with others. But charm can also
be shallow, knowing what to say without really meaning it. And he could be charming to others but lose that
capacity with you. I grew up with someone like that — he
was charming to strangers but mean to family members.

A man I dated for three months and I once talked
about what we liked about each other. I told him how
much I appreciated his thoughtfulness and generosity
with me. He said, "I've never considered myself a Prince
Charming. I try to be more of a Prince Considerate.
I work to be thoughtful of others." And he is. I think
Price Considerate is more sustaining for a relationship.

A Prince Considerate, based on the few I've had
first-hand experience with, is prone to:

💜 ***Call regularly to just say he's thinking of you,*** or
see how you're doing. (My PC called regularly
and IMed at least once a day.)

💜 ***Buy you small gifts*** to show he knows what you
like and that he cares about you. (At the movies

he excused himself and brought back chocolate for me.)

💜 ***Do thoughtful things for you spontaneously.*** (My PC regularly gave me foot massages while we chatted on the couch, or shoulder massages while we waiting in line at the movies.)

💜 ***Be thoughtful of others.*** (He brought a bottle of wine for our Halloween party hosts, as well as a high-quality chocolate bar for me!)

I think Price Considerate is more sustaining for a relationship.

💜 ***Consider what you like to do.*** (Knowing I like to see houses decorated for Halloween, he scheduled an hour's walk in a fun neighborhood near our dinner restaurant so we could enjoy the decorated houses. And he told me ahead of time to wear comfortable walking shoes!)

💜 ***Think through how a suggested activity would be for you.*** (I explained this in "Is your date sensitive to your comfort?" page 121)

💜 ***Learn your routines and plan around your regular activities.*** (PC knows what evenings I Jazzercise so suggested getting together afterwards or on other evenings.)

💜 ***Listen to your stories*** and remember what's going on in your life, and even your friends' names. (PC knew I was going to India, so suggested movies and restaurants to help acclimate me.)

So, which would you rather have, a Prince Charming or a Prince Considerate (for this discussion, you can't have both in the same guy)? Why?

Can an ambitious gal find happiness with a lackadaisical guy?

B ev, an Adventures in Delicious Dating After 40 reader, shared:

> *I met a guy a couple months ago, and I really like him. He is everything I could possibly ask for, except for one thing, he doesn't work. He is only 43 and on a pension. He told me that he was ill for two years and has not worked for two years since he got well.*

> *I like to consider myself an understanding person and am always thoughtful of the well-being of others. The fact that he hasn't worked for quite some time, and I don't see any improvement in that area, except that he says he is planning to start his own business "sometime" has me concerned.*

> *I work very hard as a single mother with 2 teens,*

and I do a lot of overtime when I can. I don't have a lot of time for pleasure, but I do try to get out as much as I can, and this guy has all the time in the world to go out to pubs and stay up all night through the week, and sleep as much through the day as he wants. All of this just doesn't sit well with me.

I really like him a lot, and he has a lot to offer as far as a relationship goes, and he has told me that he really wants me, but I am just not sure I can deal with the fact that he is unemployed and living on a very tight budget. I don't want to make my-self look materialistic, and I don't feel that I am, but I am torn and I don't know what to do.

So he's on a very tight budget but he goes to the pub multiple times a week? He has money for a few pints, but not enough to have the lifestyle that match-es yours?

This is a tough one. My ex and I had differ-ent levels of ambition and lifestyle desires. It created tension as he was happy with thrift-store furniture, for ex-ample, and I wanted nicer things. He liked to

Share what you need to feel comfortable being in a relationship

camp and hike on vacation and I'm a more bed-and-breakfast kinda gal. Money issues are one of the top topics couples argue about.

You've only been seeing him for a few months. I'd say that when it is time to have the "exclusivity" talk, you should share what you need to feel comfortable being in a relationship. Some men need a little wake up call to see that if they want to be with a great woman, they need to think beyond their own lifestyle choices. If he wants to continue living a meager life, he can do so. And you'll choose to see him along with others, decide you don't want to settle for constant financial struggles, or that you'll continue as it is now and see if he starts to shift his financial situation.

Whatever you do, don't stifle your desires without communicating. It will only cause you both frustration. Best to share your vision of what you want and both of you deciding if you can sign on to creating a life together that you both love.

Are you buff buddies?

You love working out. You are proud of your taut, fit body. You feel poorly if you don't exercise for a day. You have made this a priority in your life.

How do you feel if you have a coffee date with someone who may not share your zest for exercise? Do you dismiss him summarily, even if he has a viable excuse like a recent injury or surgery? Perhaps he's not obese, but clearly isn't an exercise fiend. Do you bid him adieu, or give him a little slack, thinking you can include hikes, walks, dancing and other physical activities in future dates to help him get in shape?

I am on the other side of this scenario. Frequently I receive emails from men whose profiles wax on about their everyday fitness regimen, perhaps accompanied by pics of their shirtless, buff selves. I am intimidated by these guys, thinking they will reject my midlife-looking body, which gets regular exercise, but has not been whipped into bathing-suit form.

So if a gym rat, marathon runner, century-riding cyclist or mountain climber inquires, I may respond, but not enthusiastically. I am afraid of a repeat of that horrible feeling when you first meet someone and you can see on his face he's disappointed. A perfunctory, requisite 20-minute coffee chat ensues, sometimes painfully, as you know you're marking time until one of you excuses him/herself gracefully.

What if a buff babe wants to keep seeing you and you know you're not his equal when it's time to reveal all? Do you put off the event as long as possible until you're sure he won't be repelled by your less-than-taut thighs — or other body parts that have been shifted by gravity? Or do you talk about your different fitness levels and invite him to do physical activities that will help you become more fit — even if you know it will be a lower pace than he's used to?

Has your guy been metro-ed?

Metro — as in metrosexual. According to Dictionary.com metrosexual, or metro, describes — "a heterosexual male who has a strong aesthetic sense and inordinate interest in appearance and style, similar to that of homosexual males."

UrbanDictionary.com includes the following description: "Mint (great) guys who are SNAGs (Sensitive New Age Guys) and follow the following rules:

1. dress hot

2. wear awesome shoes

3. have very modern haircut

4. disgusted with the thought of being with another man

5. have perfect skin and love skin products

6. love the gym

7. own nothing but designer everything

8. read style magazines often e.g, GQ

9. know how to make only the best cocktails and if they drink beer it's top-of-the-line imported

10. can't deal with a mess

I spent some time recently with a 35-year-old metro friend. He described his advising a 50-something single male pal to get a manicure to fix his ripped up and dirty fingernails. "Women like men who take care of themselves," he advised his pal. "Get a pedicure while you're at it."

Most men I've been with have never had either, nor put anything in their hair but water, or, if old enough, Brylcreem (a little dab'll do ya!). Some have learned the value of hair gel or mousse. And a few have fully embraced the metro lifestyle, using various body and hair lotions and cremes. My metro pal showed me the myriad hair products he uses. And he is a babe magnet — cute, intelligent, dresses well, and treats women right. But he's still single, although has been dating his current flame for three months.

Are you drawn to metro men? Or do you like the more rugged kind? Although a man can be rugged and still know the value of soft hair and/or skin, even though these seem at odds. What would you think of a man who fits the UrbanDictionary definition? Is there a line that is too far for you? Some men are wearing facial foundation to even out their skin tones, other midlife men are dying their hair, some use "man purses." What is acceptable to you and what isn't?

Does your date share your world view?

any months ago, I was sharing with a gal pal how I was smitten with the guy I was seeing. After stammering to answer when she asked why I liked him so much, she eventually asked, "Does he share your world view?"

I stopped in my tracks. It was a question I hadn't thought about. First, I had to think what the question meant. Next, I had to articulate my world view and look for signs of his world view. Then I compared where they matched or didn't.

So what is "world view"? Your world view is how you see the world: friendly/unfriendly, optimistically/pessimistically, people are good/people are out to get you, you are safe/you are at risk, you are treated fairly/unfairly, etc.

After this was defined, I quickly reviewed in my mind his behaviors that exemplified his world view. Within seconds, I had to answer "No" to her question.

Is it a requirement that your potential suitor share

your world view? Not necessarily. But if you are the eternal optimist and he is a constant pessimist, you will begin to drive each other crazy at some point. If he thinks all people are bad and you think generally people are good with a few bad apples, then you will experience much frustration.

I needed someone who shared more of my view of life

We could cite examples of ardent Democrats and staunch Republicans marrying and living happily. Or people with polar religious views. Or pro-lifers living with pro-choicers. However, I think these couples either are fine expressing their opposite views, or they decided not to discuss them.

My friend's question forced me to see I was smitten because of surface attributes. I needed someone who shared more of my view of life. He and I did not last long after this realization.

How important is it that a potential suitor share your world view? What elements are deal breakers and what could you be fine with disagreeing? If you haven't defined your world view, start now by listing how you see the world.

Does he share your POV?

OV — That's film-industry shorthand for "point of view shot." When the camera shows what a character sees, that's their POV. We see the scene through their eyes.

Wouldn't it be great if we could occasionally see our date's POV? To access his perspective, how he sees things? And wouldn't you like to share your view finder so he sees your perspective? It certainly would make relationships — especially the beginnings of one — much easier.

I think we typically assume the other person shares our POV — that they see and interpret events similarly to us. But the truth is, two people rarely share the same perspective about any given conversation or event. In fact, our perceptions are so unreliable "that studies have shown that individual, separate witness testimony is often flawed and parts of it can be meaningless. This can occur because of a person's faulty observation and recollection, [or] because of a person's bias…."* It's common for two eye witnesses to have very different stories with only a small overlap.

So while you and your date shared the same experience, you may have very different — perhaps 180-degree disparate — impressions of what happened.

My ex and I would frequently have different memories of an event or conversation, but he would usually chalk it up to his having a bad memory. However, in our divorce mediation when he said, "We're living like roommates" I was shocked. My perspective was we were living in a loving, supportive, sexual relationship, not without hiccups, but nothing I thought was insurmountable. This was the first time I realized we had divergent experiences of our marriage and relationship. (See "You live a rich fantasy life," in the *Check Him Out Before Going Out: Avoiding Dud Dates* book.)

In a quarrel with a guy with whom I'd had a 3-month relationship, I again had the revelation that two people can have extreme views of the same situation. One of his numerous accusations was that we only partook in activities that I wanted to do. Feeling I ensure both parties have equal say in determining activities, I asked for an example. "We only see movies you want to see." It's true that I don't like to review movies I've seen recently, and I'd watched many more than he had, but I felt we always decided on the selection jointly. I wouldn't ask him to participate in something he didn't want to do, and I expected the same from him. I was stunned that he felt I was so inflexible and selfish. During his litany of other examples of my many character flaws it was clear we had 180-degree points of view on many experiences.

I had to ask myself if I could continue in a relationship knowing that we shared so little perspective on events and motivations. His interpretation of my behaviors often — I now learned — was that I was selfish, insensitive, condescending and overbearing. I can't imagine why anyone would want to continue a relationship with anyone they perceived this way, but he said he did. I, however, didn't want to continue with someone I felt would always be interpreting whatever I did in the worst possible light — the opposite of what I intended or thought.

Luckily this extreme difference of POV came out after only three months. We'd only had one tiff prior to this row, so I had no idea his perspective was so different than mine. He had always acted as if all was hunkydory, so I had no clue anything was amiss. He was communicative so we talked about feelings and needs, but I had no idea our differently interpreting events was so rampant.

Seeing each character's POV tells you much more of the story than only seeing one. You can expect that you will sometimes have different perspectives. But when you find an extreme divergent POV is commonplace with the guy you're dating, you have to ask yourself if you want to continue costarring in this movie with him. While it might make it big at the box office, you don't want to live in "Who's Afraid of Virginia Woolf."

* Wikipedia's description of "eye witness."

Do you both have the same dating rhythm?

I had an epiphany today. It began with my being flummoxed that I hadn't heard from a guy after our dinner date — our third date — five days ago. We both said we wanted to see each other again. We'd emailed a brief "had a great time with you" the next day and that was the last I've heard from him.

Perhaps I'm spoiled. But usually after a talk like "I want to see you again" I hear from the man within a day or two wanting to set up the next outing.

Based on my experience of him last year (we'd had three dates in a few weeks before he started traveling nearly full time), I knew not to put all my beaus in one basket. So I continued emailing a man who'd contacted me early last week. He'd emailed me every day, and called Sat. to set up a coffee meeting for a few days from now. In the emails he asked if I liked the theater, opera, hiking, and what kind of restaurants I liked. He suggested some outings and after our call, emailed that he's looking forward to meeting me.

My epiphany was people have different rhythms in dating. Some think once/week contact is fine, others like daily emails and/or calls. Some like to go out once a week, others like two or three encounters each week. Some like it when you make plans in advance, ohters like spontaneous encounters.

I think it would be a good idea to clarify your preferences with someone once you decide you both want to start seeing each other. Otherwise you can be disappointed if they don't naturally fall into your desired pattern of contact.

But since I have just had this epiphany, I haven't actually tried this idea. I'm not sure when one would actually bring up this conversation. It might seem awkward on the first date, unless you are really being honest with each other about what you want in a relationship.

I like that the new guy is making regular contact, probing to find out what activities I'd like, and saying nice things. This may sound so "Duh" to you, but my experience is not many guys do this. I like that he seems to "get" dating. He seems to understand that dating can be more than just getting together for take out and a DVD, or dinner and a movie. While I haven't even met the guy yet, I already like his rhythm.

So how do you broach the subject of expectations when first dating? Or have you had a guy broach it first?

Do your activity preferences match your guy's?

re you clear on how much you like to weekly participate in activities with a sweetie? How much alone time do you want/need? How much time do you want weekly/monthly to spend with your friends and/or family without him? And when you're with your guy, optimally how many times a week do you want to do something out, versus at home?

Many online dating personality assessments ask your activity preferences. An example:

Do you prefer to go out

1) Once per week

2) 2x/week

3) 3-4x/week

4) Every night is party night

Other questions focus on specific physical activities. I've deleted guys' profiles based on their saying they spend all their free time running marathons, climbing mountains, SCUBA, mountain biking, back-country skiing, working out and playing team sports. I get tired just reading about all this physical activity! While I'm not a slug, I'm also not an iron woman.

When you're beginning to date someone, one of the first questions to ask is "What do you like to do for fun?" Of course, what one likes to do is often different than what you actually do. Men have told me they like to go to live theater, concerts, fine dining, wine tasting, dancing, first-run movies, lectures, comedy clubs, etc. However, when dating them, their idea of a "date" is to rent a DVD and get take out. Or occasionally dinner out and a movie. That's it. I've been flummoxed at why a guy doesn't make any effort to arrange for us to do what he says he likes to do.

What one likes to do is often different than what you actually do

One of my frustrations of being single is not having a ready-made activity partner. My friends are available for some activities, but most are coupled so have limited time to spend with buddies. I see first-run flicks once in a while with some gal pals. I like to see the world, try new things, re-experience old favorites, and I prefer to do those activities with friends, ideally a sweetie. Yes, there are organized activity groups, dance classes, ranger-led wildflower hikes, and other classes or singles-focused events. An experience is richer to me when I can discuss it with someone during and/or afterwards to share each others perspectives and insights.

Imagine my delight when I found a man I dated for three months liked to do — and initiated — fun stuff! In seven days together (he visited three times from out of state) in a month we:

- Picnicked and walked on the beach (twice, different beaches)

- Went square dancing

- Visited a Blues club

- Taken a hike in a nearby regional park, along with a picnic

- Dined at a Japanese restaurant

- Played tourist in a nearby city

- Breakfasted out

- Walked in my neighborhood

- Cooked dinner together

- Viewed an indy flick at the local film festival

- And yes, snuggled on the coach in front of a fire and watched a DVD

♥ And we also just kicked back, took naps and relaxed.

When I visited him for a week and he's arranged:

♥ Visiting one of my friends for a horseback ride and dinner

♥ Attending his professional awards banquet

♥ Viewing the local tulip festival

♥ Dining with his friends and his kids

♥ Overnighting at his favorite beach inn.

And he worked four days during the week I was there! If we lived in the same town, we would not have crammed so much in. But we liked to make maximum use of our together time. So my activity needs were being met, both for frequency and variety, and with a fun, loving partner.

Does this sound like too much "doing" to you? Too little? Do you like variety, routine, or a mix?

When you know your activity frequency and variety desires, communicate them to your guy early on and see if you have similar wants. If he agrees with your preferences, yet doesn't want to participate in ideas you offer, nor take initiative to do anything interesting, discuss the disconnect and see if he's willing to step up — and out — a bit more.

Does he fit in your world?

For a relationship to work long term, I believe it's important that you are able to fit into each other's world. Not that you have to live parallel lives with the same profession, income, hobbies, etc.

But is important that you can easily slip into each other's activities, gracefully converse with the other's counterparts and dress appropriately for the occasion.

This seems common sense, I know. And you'd think that if you are drawn to a man he would automatically fit into your world. However, I can tell you from experience that just because you get along well with him, it doesn't mean he will meld with your friends and/or colleagues.

Years ago I took the crazy psychiatrist I was dating to my film group's small potluck dinner and movie viewing. I was stunned at how loud and combative his comments were to the others. And his table manners were atrocious — he piled high the various dishes as if he were the only one to share the dish. He didn't have great table manners when we ate at my house, but when we are among strangers we usually put on our best manners. Not him.

Another early beau accompanied me to a party. We mixed and mingled, but I noticed that he turned nearly every conversation back to himself, not asking others anything about what they were sharing. He didn't do this with me, so I was surprised to witness this boorish behavior. At another small party, he took over the group conversation and "held court" with his comments, long past when others tried to have side conversations. He'd call them by name and say, "Listen to this..." and prattle on, relishing being the center of attention. I quickly decided it was time to go, although he protested.

Before I was married, I dated a man who was loving and sweet to me. But when we were around others, he would talk incessantly about things he knew little about but acted like he was an expert. If he learned someone scuba dove, he talked as if he also dove. He'd never donned a tank in his life. I found this too awkward and didn't invite him to parties.

Other dates have showed up at events inappropriately attired, even though I informed them of the event's level of dress. Either they didn't care or thought their underdressed attire would be OK. They didn't realize their inappropriateness would reflect on me. One came to a dressy cocktail party in a ill-fitting casual sport coat and sneakers.

When a beau and I talked about why I didn't respond to his first overture when his only picture posted was of him in sunglasses and a t-shirt. I explained that if he'd posted a picture in the cashmere polo shirt he wore to our first date I would have responded. Was I being shallow? Perhaps. But part of our decision of if we want to get to know someone or not is assessing if they will fit into our world. If there is too much disparity, it will be harder. It can work, but it is some effort on both your parts.

In an episode of "Sex and the City," lawyer Miranda invites her new beau to her office party. As a bartender, the only suit he owns is corduroy. They realize this won't work, but he can't afford a new suit. She decides to buy him one. It's awkward for him to accept this, but he knows he must if he is going to be integrated into her world.

If there is too much disparity, it will be harder.

One of the things I've liked about dating is being brought into a world I might not otherwise experience. I like trying new things, so if a man has different interests and hobbies, I'm generally willing to try his activities — at least once. However, if he only frequents biker bars or the opera, we're not a good fit. Although I'd probably accompany him to either at least once to see if I liked it.

So when my beau stated that he was going to buy a new suit to accompany me to some business social functions, I knew he wanted to fit into my world. He has the manners and social graces to fit easily — not that my pals are hoity-toity. But it is nice to know that he would look the part as well as engage others with an equal give and take.

What are ways you access if a new guy will fit into your world? How long do you wait to take a guy you're dating to social events with friends or colleagues? Have you had a guy not invite you to events you know he attends that would be acceptable for a date (e.g., holiday or birthday parties).

What's your communication compatibility?

For threee days I visited a relative I love dearly. However, it drove me crazy that she incessantly second guessed what I was doing. When I was packing, she suggested other ways to pack. She asked questions that I thought were superfluous (e.g., "What did you have for lunch?" "Will you and your boyfriend get married?" "What is your ex-husband doing now?")

And she displayed one of the most annoying habits I know — not self editing. She exemplifies that phrase, "She has never had a thought not worth sharing." So she tells great details about others we don't know nor care about. And constantly chatters her stream of consciousness, no matter how banal.

But I love her dearly so put up with it, reminding myself she has a good heart and means well. And I was grateful I didn't stay five days like last time.

It made me think about how important communication compatibility is in dating.

I've also experienced the opposite — being out with a guy who was so uncommunicative it was a lot of work to make any conversation. He gave me one-word answers to questions and never asked me a thing.

So where are you on this continuum? Are you a non-stop talker? If so, do you like quiet men? Or are you more reserved, and like someone who is more verbal? Or maybe if you don't like to talk much, you like someone quiet, too.

Are you a non-stop talker?

One of the things I love about my sweetie is it seems we have the same talking tolerance. I don't find he talks too much nor too little. And I hope he feels the same way!

You should be clear on your preference so you can screen out those who would get on your nerves before you even meet. Phone calls can tell you a lot, but some habits don't appear until you're face to face.

What's your kissing quotient?

I had six dates with a guy, but only one passionate kiss — on the fifth date! Before that I got pecks hello and goodbye. I began to wonder if he thought of me as a pal — or worse, his sister! But he treated me and touched me in ways that said otherwise. I'd think, "This guy just doesn't like kissing," but before we even met he asked me if I liked to kiss and I said yes. So I don't think that's the problem.

Only one other guy took more dates — six — to passionately smooch. Other guys have locked lips too much and too soon — some within minutes of meeting me. So I've begun to wonder if each person has a kissing quotient. And you have to work it out with potential partners so both person's kissing needs are met.

There are several kissing quotient criteria:

💜 ***How soon*** — After first meeting someone, at what point do you feel it is appropriate to passionately kiss? This can vary widely depending on the person and the attraction you have to each other. However, do you have some general guidelines? Tyra Banks has said she never kisses on the first date, and if a guy tries to plant one on her lips, she turns her cheek. She wants him to really want to kiss her during the second date!

♥ *Frequency* — Some people like to kiss a lot — both pecks and passionately. Do you like a lot of kissing, some, or hardly any? Some people can interpret lots of kissing as lots of attraction. Others feel it shows neediness and clinginess — or horniness!

♥ *Timing* — Do you like kissing anywhere you feel drawn to your partner — on the street, in the movies, in a store, or do you prefer private necking — in the car and at home? Or do you like making out only in bed?

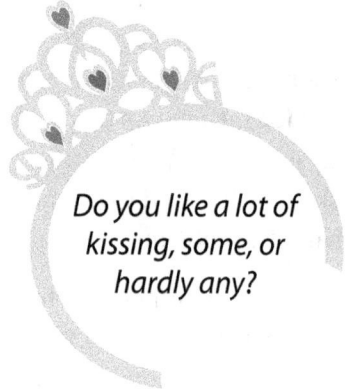

Do you like a lot of kissing, some, or hardly any?

♥ *Duration* — Some folks like to kiss for hours. Others for only a few minutes. What's the length of time you're comfortable necking?

♥ *Style* — Some people have no kissing foreplay. No nibbles or suggestive busses. They just start full bore. If you like nibbles and he's a "full court press" guy, there's a mismatch. I've even tried to teach guys how I liked to be kissed, with not a lot of success.

Of course, all of this depends on how much you enjoy canoodling with the other person. If you don't consider him a good kisser, you're probably not going to extend your lip-locking activities.

Hmmm. Maybe my beau du jour doesn't like my kisses! Or maybe he is afraid they will make him get weak knees and he'll lose his decorum!

Kisses do tell

Women place more emphasis on the first kiss than men do. We use it as part of determining if we want to see the man again or not.

University at Albany researchers Susan M. Hughes, Marissa A. Harrison, and Gordon G. Gallup, Jr. recently published their findings on kissing in an Evolutionary Psychology article.

They discovered they were no longer interested after they kissed

This was another study using only college students, 1,041 in fact. So I'm not sure that we can assume that this information applies to midlife daters. But it does seem consistent with my experience — a sample size of one.

Many of the college students reported having been attracted to someone, then discovered they were no longer interested after they kissed them for the first time.

"In other words," said Gallup, an evolutionary psy-

chologist, "While many forces lead two people to connect romantically, the kiss, particularly the first kiss, can be a deal breaker."

Exactly. In "In search of the elusive good kisser" (page 13) I share the challenge of finding men who fit my criteria in this area. As I've gone out with 80 men now, although I haven't kissed all of them, I've kissed enough that I've begun to relax my standards a bit. But if a man is such a sloppy kisser I need a towel afterwards, or has other kissing habits I find off putting, it will be a factor in my decision to see him again.

Kissing as a determinant of another date is mostly true just for women. Men said they saw kissing an a way to gain sexual favors or to make up after a problem. But women use kissing to assess the status of the relationship. Most females shared they would never engage in sex without kissing. However, men would; men said they'd have sex with someone who was not a "good" kisser.

The study showed that it was more common for males than females to initiate French kissing. In my experience, many men don't gauge accurately if the woman is ready for that intimacy or not. They go there too soon, which can be a turn off rather than a turn on.

What do you think about first kisses? Does the man or woman generally initiate? And do you use a first passionate kiss to determine if you're interested in continuing seeing your date?

Is he a "soft place to fall"?

r. Phil uses the term "a soft place to fall" to express a safe space to be vulnerable. He frequently asks troubled couples if they each provide a soft place to fall for the other.

When you've dated a guy for a little while, do you feel you can be vulnerable with him, admitting your fears and doubts? Sharing your setbacks and disappointments in yourself, your job, your life?

Or do you feel you need to be guarded, never letting on that your life is anything less than optimal, lest he think you are a mess and dump you fearing he'll have to straighten it out? While some men relish the opportunity to be the White Knight, even seeking out women who regularly need a lot of help, others bail at the first sign of anything amiss.

Nobody has a trouble-free life. No matter how rosy, I bet there are aspects of your life that aren't perfect, or could at least be improved. Maybe it's something closeted, that he'd never know about if you didn't tell him. Perhaps it's a strained relationship with a family member, or a financial setback, or a chronic minor health challenge.

I don't recommend revealing these in the first few dates. But after you've been with the guy a few times and begun to trust him and get closer, are you comfortable disclosing these hitches? If not, ask yourself why. Is it that he gets upset hearing your challenges? Or he immediately tries to fix the problem, rather than just listening to

Does he get upset hearing your challenges?

you? Or he responds by telling you that you "shouldn't feel that way," or it was "stupid to get yourself in that situation," or "Here's what you should do…." This is not a soft place to fall.

Let him know what you need: "I want to share something I'm not proud of, but I think you should know. You may be tempted to try to help me brainstorm a solution, but right now I'd really like you to just listen and hold me. After I've shared my thoughts, I'll tell you when — and if — I'm ready for us to go into problem-solving mode." If he ignores you, remind him of your request. He may not have had anyone be this clear on what she wanted and he doesn't have any muscle built up on how to just listen.

And ask yourself if you are a "soft place to fall" for him. Many men don't like to be vulnerable, so if he shares something that he's not proud of, be gentle with him. Acknowledge the courage it took to admit this to you and allow him to share without your problem solving or being judgmental. Ask him what he'd like from you right now to feel supported. If the wound is deep, he may start crying, which is very hard for many man to let a woman see. Especially a woman he's interested in romantically.

So work on your "soft landing" skills, and allow him to work on his as well. These are muscles some of us don't use a lot, so the first few landings may be a bit bumpy, but stick with it!

Is his diet a problem for you?

Or is yours a problem for him?

In past writings, I've explored how the way a man eats can be problematic (eats salad with his fingers, chews with his mouth full, picks up pork chops with his hands in a nice restaurant). But we've not discussed how *what* he eats — or doesn't eat — may be a problem, too.

Generally, I'm for being as forgiving, understanding and tolerant as you can possibly be about minor mismatches. "So," you may be asking, "what do I care what he eats as long as we match in other areas? Aren't we being a bit petty here?"

Aren't we being a bit petty here?

Yes, for many it doesn't really matter. And if you've only dated men who eat generally what you eat, then you don't see how this might be a challenge.

Here's where it becomes dicey — you only eat healthy fare — fish and vegetables, maybe organic chicken. He is a fast-food king. Yes, you can get salads and grilled chicken at most fast food places, and fish, albeit typically fried. So while you don't mind eating a Wendy's salad once in a while, it's not your preference. But if he nearly always prefers fast food, you can see the argument coming.

While the above can be a true challenge, it's not really restaurant eating that tests your relationship's mettle. You can generally get something both of you will eat, even if you have to order something not on the menu.

While you would think cooking at home would be even easier, it isn't always. My ex dabbled in vegetarianism over the years and I supported his choice by cooking along his preferences. If I wanted a chicken breast or occasional steak, I'd cook one. Not that this was a big problem, but if I wanted to roast a whole chicken, I ate it for a week, or invited friends over to share, or froze some.

But when we ate out, previously we'd often share an entree, wanting to be mindful of our waistlines. So when he was vegetarian, I was my making more modifications to my preferences, not him. When you love someone you learn to make compromises. But in this area, it seemed I was the one who was making the compromises, not him.

One man decided he was going to lose 50 pounds soon after we began dating. He stopped eating anything white, so when I went to his house, we didn't eat pasta, rice, or sourdough bread. I know this is a healthy way to eat and went along with it as I, too, would love to lose weight. But I wasn't as committed to it as he was (he had heart problems and was highly motivated), although I know it would have been good for me. But I longed for some of the forbidden whites, even in small portions.

We didn't go together long enough for me to lose weight on this spartan diet!

I dated a vegan for a while and finding dinner solutions that we could both enjoy became a challenge. So we'd fix separate things, or I'd supplement the meager salad with a chicken breast or cheese. And darn, we didn't go together long enough for me to lose weight on this spartan diet!

What if he's said he wants to lose weight and yet he continues to eat high-fat, fried, unhealthy food? You can say something and he might see your trying to help as nagging. No one likes food police.

Or what if you want to lose weight or eat healthily and he continues to serve you high-calorie foods or suggest going to unhealthy restaurants? I remember visiting a friend in New Orleans and he took me to his favorite restaurant. I scrutinized the menu, trying to find something that wasn't deep-fat fried. I finally asked that the fried salmon be broiled instead. My friend's order was delivered — a foot-high fried-food mountain of shrimp, crawdads, catfish, okra, French fries, and other Louisiana fare. It was hard for me to watch, especially knowing he had health challenges.

Or what if you have developed a sophisticated palate and enjoy fine foods and wine? But your guy is a beer and pizza aficionado. Unless you both realize you have to compromise a bit, or agree to only go to your very favorite places with friends who share your tastes, this will be a problem.

Have you experienced any food polarity problems with your dates? If so, how have you worked it out?

Is he assertive enough for you?

In women's dating stories of budding relationships gone awry, there are two common themes:

1. The man was too aggressive too early.

2. The man wasn't assertive enough to say what he needed, or make requests for minor modifications of adaptable behaviors, so he went poof.

Number 1 is pretty self-explanatory — he got too physical or sexual too early and that turned off the woman.

So let's explore #2. Of course, these issues can apply to both men and women, but we're going to focus on the man's behavior.

I've learned I need an assertive man for me to be happy. I have to be assertive in my business life and prefer to not have to take care of both of us in a relationship. In fact, there are times I relish having my guy take care of me. When he does this I let him know I really like it.

So when he doesn't have the ability to step up, it stands out. Let me share an example.

On the way home from a concert with a man I'd dated for a month, he in his tux, I in evening attire, we weren't ready to call it a night. I'm a sucker for views, so suggested we stop for a nightcap at the nearby hilltop hotel with a fantastic vantage point to watch the lights twinkling in the distance. We discovered the bar was in the basement, so no view. However, the restaurant had a fabulous view. At 10:00 it was nearly empty.

We asked the hostess for one of the several empty tables near the window for dessert and a drink. She pointed to tables with no view and said we could sit there. I politely said we were hoping for a nice view and could we have one of the window tables. She said she'd check.

She came back and said no, we couldn't be seated there for just dessert. My date turned to leave. I nicely asked who she consulted and she said the waiter. I knew the waiter would not want to waste his energy on lower-tabbed dessert/drink customers, but would hold out for full-dinner ones, even though most people had dined by that hour.

I was not happy with this answer, so I calmly asked if she'd bring the manager over for us to consult with. She went to the manager, who said, "No problem" and we were promptly seated next to the window facing the great view.

Since I'd waited a few beats before speaking up to see if my date would take the lead, I asked if I'd stepped on his toes. He said, "Absolutely not. I would never have had the courage to ask for the window table in the first place. I would have settled on the first non-view ones she wanted to steer us to. I would have never asked to see the manager."

I knew then that we were not long-term material.

Was what I did over the top? I don't think so. I was polite and pleasant the whole time, but unwilling to let the hostess's and waiter's decisions stand without exploring all the options I could think of. Had the restaurant been full, I would have understood. But it was not. And the waiter would get some tip, which was better than having an empty table with no tip. So I saw it as a win/win solution. But my date's mind didn't think that way. Perhaps it wasn't important to him, but since it was important to me, I'd expect some effort to then have it be important to him. Just as I would make something important that was important to him become important to me.

How important is assertiveness to you in a man you're seeing? If he isn't, do you mind taking the lead most of the time? If you'd like him to step up more often, how do you communicate this without him feeling like a wuss?

Make sure to download your free eBook Attract Your Next Great Mate: Dating Advice From Top Relationship Experts *at www.DatingGoddess.com/freebie*

R-E-S-P-E-C-T

Otis Redding wrote it.

Aretha Franklin belted it.

The song says all the writer/singer wants is respect from his/her partner. Just a little respect.

Have you ever felt someone you were dating didn't respect you? Maybe he chastised you, second guessed you or told you your actions or decisions were wrong?

Or have you noticed your own lack of respect in the man? He acted in ways you thought were juvenile, or made decisions you felt weren't thought through? You may have kept these observations to yourself or you may have said something. Even if you thought you were keeping it to yourself, I can guarantee the disrespect seeped out.

You may be saying, "Respect is a deal breaker. Why bother even mentioning it?"

Because some of us were raised in environments with little respect. Disrespect was the norm. So if we give or receive disrespect, we think that is how relationships are supposed to be.

I've been on both sides. I'm not proud to admit I haven't always hidden it if someone I've been dating for a while does something I think is immature. Of course, the outcome is predictably bad. It can — and usually does — cause a chasm in the relationship.

Respect is critical for a healthy relationship. Not that we don't all periodically do things that are not fully thought through, or naive or even, in retrospect, foolish. But to have this pointed out by the person we're wanting most to impress is not a good thing. Not at all. When we discover our folly, there is usually enough self-flagellation that no one else needs to remind us of our stupidity.

And if we don't think what we said/did/decided is dumb, we really don't want to hear that the other thought it was. We feel disrespected. Which no one wants to feel.

If you can talk about this feeling of disrespect calmly and rationally with your guy, great. It is hard to do without one or both of you getting defensive. The person showing disrespect feels justified, and the person who said/did what caused the reaction feels justified.

But it is important to note when you have feelings of being disrespected by the man you're seeing, as well as when you feel he's made a dumb decision. The more frequently either of these occur, the more the bells should be going off in your head — and not the sweet chime of a dainty dinner bell. These are fire station alarms clanging warning you to wake up and get out of the building (AKA relationship)!

Is he emotionally mature?

I was sharing with the man I'd been dating for three months that many midlife women complain that the men they date are lacking emotional availability.

> *"Do you mean emotional availability or emotional maturity?" he asked.*

> *"Hmm," I responded, "I'm not sure I can define the difference. From the brief research I did on the"Net, it seems emotional unavailability is being too busy, sick, tired or preoccupied with other things. Energy, time and focus are all taken with other priorities." (See "Emotional unavailability," in the Embracing Midlife Men: Insights Into Curious Behaviors book.)*

> *"Yes, I think that is a good definition of emotional unavailability and I think that can be true for both genders. It's a way of protecting yourself from potential hurt, as you don't allow anyone to get near you."*

"That makes sense. Let's define emotional maturity."

"My definition is someone who takes very few things personally. Whatever happens doesn't necessarily reflect on them. For example, if someone cuts them off on the freeway, the other driver isn't out to get them."

"Or their boss' bad mood isn't caused by them. They are grounded, centered and able to give others the benefit of the doubt. They aren't paranoid."

"Yes, and they are conscious of how others' behaviors that trigger them are a chance to look at their old hurts, not to make the other person wrong."

"Do you know how rare that is? Most of my friends are like that, but I find many of the people I interact with in my profession want to blame others for their problems. I catch myself doing it sometimes."

"Yes, I know that is a common response to challenges. Most people don't want to look at their responsibility in reacting the way they do. But you have a lot of emotional maturity. How do you think you got it?"

"By lots of personal work, therapy and personal growth workshops. It isn't easy facing your demons and seeing how you are the orchestrator of your own problems. How do you think you've gained your emotional maturity?"

"Similarly. I was in pain for a long time during

and after my marriage. Finally, a good friend suggested I get some help, and when I did I saw how I contributed to the downfall of my marriage, when I'd just blamed my ex before. I began to get new skills and it changed my relationships with friends, coworkers and my kids, so I wanted more."

How do you know where you are on an emotional maturity continuum? I don't know that we could accurately assess ourselves. I think we'd need to ask those who are closest to us, and be willing to hear their answers, even if the scores are low. After all, if you get upset, that validates their score! Paradoxically, an emotionally mature person would be able to deal with low scores.

Just as importantly, how do you assess your date's score? By watching how he reacts to others, especially when something hasn't gone well. If the waiter brings the wrong order, is slow, or spills something, is your date aggressively confrontational? If something needs to be said, is he professional and not overly emotional? How does he respond if someone cuts him off on the freeway? Does he ignore it, or curse loudly? Watch for signs of emotional immaturity in the beginning, when he is theoretically on his best behavior, as it will only increase as he lets his guard down.

How do you assess your date's emotional maturity?

Since we know it is very difficult to change another, (see "Ignore dating rule #1 at your peril") and, in my experience, nearly impossible to get someone to increase their maturity level unless they are internally motivated to do so, best to let someone go who isn't at the level you desire. And if you find out you are lower on the continuum than you'd like, decide how you can help yourself move up the scale and begin now. You'll then attract those who are also higher on the ladder.

Does he want a "mommy"?

Some midlife women complain that some men they've dated want someone to take care of them — a mommy. Of course, in an Oedipal twist, they also want her to perform in the bedroom, assuming he still can.

Being a mother figure isn't all bad if that is what you like. Many women like nurturing and caring for others. But it does upset the transactional analysis concept that we behave in Parent, Adult and Child modes. Eric Berne's theory is that the most evolved relationship is one where both people treat each other like adults.

Some couples' relationships, however, are built on both taking on Adult/Parent behaviors for various tasks. Even some 21st-Century women expect the man be the Parent in the economic area where he is the primary breadwinner. The trade off is she takes on the Parent role in the caretaking/housekeeping area.

So what are the signs a guy is just looking for someone to take care of him? Here's a list of somewhat obvious signs. (Any of these alone is not evidence of his wanting to be mommied, but if there are many of these signs, cut the apron strings.)

♥ *He lets you do all the cooking, cleaning, laundry and domestic duties.* If you suggest he help, he makes excuses, including "I don't do it as well as you." He conveniently "forgets" to do the tasks you request to share household chores. When he does something that he deems your job, he makes a big deal out of it wanting accolades.

♥ *He behaves in child-like ways.* He leaves his clothes on the floor, doesn't take initiative for household repairs, doesn't manage his bills, may neglect his hygiene or appearance.

> *His idea of cuddling is for you to enwrap him in your arms.*

♥ *He shows submissiveness.* Instead of his putting his arm around you, he takes your arm and puts it around his shoulders. His idea of cuddling is for you to enwrap him in your arms.

♥ *He gets defensive* if you give him any constructive criticism. He may get angry, surly or even pout.

- *He shows off,* calling for you to look at what he's done. "Honey, come listen to how the car now hums since I tuned it."

- *He expects you to make the majority of "adult" decisions for you both,* e.g., investments, bill paying, major household improvements.

Although I typically avoid mommy-seekers like the plague, I stupidly went with one for 6 weeks. When I examined my role in my 20-year marriage, I saw I was more mommy-like than I prefer. I decided I no longer wanted to be a mother figure to another adult. I'm so adamant about this concept of not wanting to be a care-taker, I have an auto-watering yard, and refuse to get a bird bath, bird feeder or pet — anything that needs my frequent care!

What are signs you've seen that show a man wants to be mommied?

Does he "get" you?

The dictionary has many meanings for the word "get." This discussion is about the informal term for "understand." But I think""get" goes beyond just understanding.

A colleague and I were discussing how some colleagues were misinterpreting my motivations for an action. He said, "They don't really get you."

We all want a mate who understands us and "gets" us. While "understand" and "get" are used interchangeably, many of us interpret "get" with a deeper meaning. In discussing this with my friend Ken, I shared that a distinction for me is if understanding is followed by action, then s/he "gets" it/me. In other words, if someone "gets" you they show it in some action.

In the examples above, Larry felt I "got" him because I could discuss his work and his ultimate motivations and philosophies behind why he does what he does. My colleagues didn't "get" me because they misinterpreted my motivations negatively.

Here's another example. I know my favorite auntie likes to talk to me every two weeks. I could simply let her call me every other week. But I""get" her, so I put it on my calendar to call her every other week. She is delighted to hear from me and knows I'm thinking of her and want to show her I care.

My sweetie "gets" me like no man before him. A little example: He knows it's important for me that we make contact each day, so he sends me a "Good morning, Goddess" email for me to read first thing. I respond, as I know it's important for him to hear from me as well. And we talk at least once to check in. Sometimes I send him a "Good morning" email before I go to bed so he'll have a message from me when he awakens. We are learning how to show the other we "get" them.

I think "getting" someone takes time. "Getting" someone can include learning what they like, how they think, what motivates them, what their wounds and triggers are, and what actions show you care. In "Do you love how he loves you?" we explored how to discuss how you show and feel love. When you""get" someone you're dating, you work to give them what that will make them happy and reduce the actions that will trigger sadness or upset.

What is the distinction of "get" for you? How do you know if the guy you're dating "gets" you? And how do you know if you "get" him?

In boyfriend you trust?

A gal pal shared a concern about her boyfriend of two months. "He's still has a very strong relationship with both his ex-wife and his last girlfriend. He's been apart from his ex-girlfriend a year after a year-long relationship. And he's been divorced from his ex-wife three years after a two-year marriage.

> "His ex-girlfriend comes over to his place and bakes cookies for him and his friends, and cat sits in his home while he's away. He insists that they are just friends now, but their closeness bothers me."

> "Do you trust him?" I ask.

> "Yes."

> "Then what's the problem?"

> "I'm uncomfortable since my last boyfriend insisted he was over his last girlfriend, then he left me to go back with her."

Aha. She doesn't trust that this new one won't do what her ex-beau did to her. She's projecting her insecurities onto her new man. She knows this is her issue and she doesn't want to be one of those controlling, paranoid women who kills a good relationship because of her issues. But she can't seem to shake this feeling of unrest.

💜 "If he really cared about me, he'd honor my discomfort with his closeness to these past relationships and cut back on his contact with them," she said.

💜 "Or, you could work on your trust issues and be happy that he left these relationships with such good will that he's able to maintain friendships. Many people leave relationships with bitterness and resentment on one or both sides. It says a lot about him that he's able to maintain good relations with these former love interests.

💜 "Can you believe him when he says he's over them and has no desire to be with either of them again? If you aren't able work through your trust issues, you'll have a hard time with this in any relationship."

One of my past beaus was so friendly with his ex-wife they exchanged dating stories and advice. I've maintained friendships with several of my former sweeties. My ex-husband was so cordial with

My ex's first wife once stayed with us for a week.

his first wife she once came and stayed with us for a week, and she and I spent the day together shopping. So keeping a good relationship with an ex can be done. And I understand that it can sometimes evolve into a reconciliation.

Trust is basic to a relationship. If you don't see any signs that he is lying yet you still don't trust him, you'll poison the bond. No one wants to be around someone who is questioning your word.

Have you been in a situation like this where your sweetie was still friendly with his ex? If so, how did you handle it if you had any concerns?

Is your guy "spoilable"?

We're usually more concerned with dealing with a man who is spoiled — self-centered, immature, and thoughtless. Ditch those guys immediately.

I'm talking about the opposite — someone who is so other-focused that it is hard for him to receive.

Most of us — at least me — like to be spoiled once in a while. It feels great to receive without the necessity of reciprocating — at least immediately. I think it's why spas are so popular, especially among women. We typically give so much to others every day, that at the spa we can just kick back and receive. Of course, we remunerate in tips and fees, but it seems we get way more than we pay.

It is hard for some people to receive without needing to reciprocate. That's why birthdays are great — you can give (or receive) and there is no concern about the favor/gift being immediately matched. The only expectation is a sincere thank you. And if the gift is truly liked, a big smile, hug, etc. will telegraph the appreciation.

It feels great to give something to someone you know the other will really enjoy. I work to notice what a sweetie likes and give him more of it.

Recently, I told Prince Considerate how much I appreciated his spoiling me and want to learn what makes him feel spoiled. He said, "That will be interesting. I don't really know, as no one has ever spoiled me." That includes his mother, ex-wife and past girlfriends. He's mastered the art of giving, but has little competency in receiving. Not that he eschews receiving massages, favorite foods or compliments, but it is harder to be given to than to receive.

Some would say that not everyone needs to be spoiled. Perhaps. But if you can't receive readily and without feeling you must repay in kind, there is a block to receiving love. Love, in part, is feeling special around another person. Receivin — even spoiling — is part of that.

What have you noticed about spoiling men? Are the ones who are good at spoiling you equally as good at receiving spoiling?

(See related section, "Are you open to receiving?" in the *Date or Wait: Are You Ready for Mr. Great?* book.)

Is your date sensitive to your comfort?

n "Before agreeing to a weekend getaway, clarify expectations" (in the *Ironing Out Dating Wrinkles: Work Through Challenges Without Getting Steamed* book) I shared how I've learned to ask better questions before going on an outing. So I asked a few when a man I'd gone out with 5 times in a month asked if I wanted to accompany him and his photography club to a horse show. "What happens at the show?" "How long would we be there?" What will be your responsibilities entail?"

But as the event approached, I realized I really didn't know how the day might unfold, what to wear and bring. I asked him to paint me a picture of what he imagined would happen. He said he and his club members would be out among the horses taking pictures to back up the official photographer and get additional candid shots. I would be outside in the bleachers watching the barrel races and other activities. Since it was autumn, I should bring warm clothes, umbrella, rain coat, bleacher pad, hat and book. We'd have lunch from the on-site vendors and he'd check on me periodically. Afterward we'd have a nice dinner nearby.

This date was having less appeal. After explaining the day, he realized this without my saying a word. He said that if that not wasn't my idea of a good time, then he could always go with his club and we'd hook up in the evening for dinner. I was appreciative that he suggested this out so I didn't have to. I told him that when I accepted his invitation I envisioned we'd have more time together. So spending the day alone in the cold and possibly rainy weather was not what I'd hoped for. I wanted to spend the day with him, not seeing him from afar.

He was sensitive to what would be my experience of the event and proactively suggested a more suitable alternative. Unlike my experience detailed in "Teed off by weekend getaway with golf addict," this guy was thoughtful and sensitive to my needs.

> *I wanted to spend the day with him, not seeing him from afar*

While you may think this would be a no brainer, I've found it rare to have a man think through how the experience he's suggesting would be for me. One that plans ahead — brings a blanket, a thermos of a warm drink, an extra hat or gloves, etc., — seems to be even rarer. I once went on a drizzly-day date to a professional baseball game. My date brought nothing but his jacket. I had a towel to wipe down the seats and a blanket to keep us warm. Is it that women are more wired to think things through? Is it our motherliness, even if we aren't a mom? Or is it that women value comfort more than men? I'm not sure.

I am sure that I appreciate a man who thinks through an event and includes my enjoyment in his calculations.

What have you noticed about thinking through things in dating? Are men more, less or equally apt to think and plan ahead? Or is that more a woman's thing?

Is your guy's loving muscle strong?

I'm talking about his willingness and ability to regularly show caring, affection and love, whether to you or others.

I've noticed that men I'm dating who are used to showing their love to their parents, children, friends, church members, etc., are more able to express their love to me. They are unembarrassed about conveying their caring. They have developed a habit of communicating their affection either through touch, acts of thoughtfulness, or verbalizing their feelings.

When a person hasn't shown their caring for another for a while, their love muscle atrophies. I've dated men who behaved awkwardly about showing their affection'— either too much too soon or too little. They only expressed ambivalence or even disdain toward family members and had few — if any — close friends. These men can either come on too needy or too aloof.

After long-single men friends have a girlfriend for a while, I've noticed they treat me with more care.

They seem to better understand that women like to be treated kindly, even if colleagues, not love interests. Not all men understand this, of course, even those who've been partnered for a while. But some men do seem to up their caring quotient.

The man I'm currently seeing regularly gives his time and caring to infirm members of his former profession. He's part of a group of able-bodied retires who visit the homes, hospital or hospice of those who need companionship. They champion their compatriots' chores by painting their houses, repairing fences, or performing overdue yard work for those who have fallen on hard times. When he tells me of his day's activities it is always with humility and gratefulness for the service these elders have done in the past. He has a huge giving heart which shows up in how he expresses his affection for me.

While the stereotype is that women have a strong loving muscle from taking care of children, mates, siblings, parents and friends, just like any muscle it could always be strengthened. The beauty of flexing your loving muscle is no matter who you use it on it will be stronger and available for use when the right man comes into your life. Who could you flex your loving muscle with today?

Is your date trainable?

Sometimes I'm asked why I don't always speak up when a date does something I don't like. I weigh several things:

Do I care enough about this relationship to put effort in trying to improve it?

> If it is a one-time coffee date with someone I can see isn't a good match, then I don't say anything. Or if I have been on the fence and am weighing if I want to keep seeing him, when the scale tips to "no," why say something? Perhaps it's just a problem for me, but the next gal won't be bothered by the behavior.

Is the act something that is core to his personality, so isn't likely to be changed?

> The golf addict's (see the *Ironing Out Dating Wrinkles: Work Through Challenges Without Getting Steamed* book) self-absorption was too core to him that it would have taken more than I wanted to invest in changing him. And after spending more time with him I decided he didn't have enough compelling characteristics for me

127

to think it would be worth the effort for him to be a match.

Will *he hear it without getting defensive?*

Some of his reaction will be based on how I make my request or comment. Some men have become defensive when I've made what I thought was a simple request in a pleasant tone nicely phrased. If I have evidence that he'll get defensive, then I will pick my battles carefully. Of course, if he gets defensive easily, he's not going to be around long!

If it is something simple, I will say something if I care about deepening the relationship.

For example, if I'd decided I wanted to continue seeing him, I would have said something when the golf addict wore his golf cap during lunch inside the cafe. Or I would have made a comment or request to the date who watched TV over my shoulder at dinner. Or the one who didn't walk me to my door when bringing me home from a date. While these could be considered "core" inconsiderate behaviors, if a guy hasn't been with a woman in a while, I think he forgets (or perhaps never knew) how to be considerate.

Women friends say, "You need to say something or he'll never learn and he'll keep treating other women this way." First, what seems inconsiderate to me, may not to another woman. In sharing the instance of they guy dropping me off without walking me to my door, a gal pal said that wouldn't bother her in the least. And she hates having the chair pulled out for her, doors opened, and assistance with her coat. So different strokes.

Second, I don't think it is my place in early dates to train someone. If a successful, educated, midlife man isn't astute enough to understand common courtesies, I don't think I should be training him. I don't want to be his mother. If his parents didn't train him, he needs to be smart enough to know that his behaviors are critical in both personal and business relationships, and he needs to have become educated in how to best treat people.

If we have dated a few times and it's something important to me and I'll say something. One younger man who declared he wanted to be my boyfriend, never helped with my coat, even when I was dressed up. One day I said, "Do you know how to help a woman with her coat?" He said. "No." I said, "Then you're going to learn." On the third date, another began to eat his salad with his fingers. I suggested he use the fork.

In "When do you tell your date about irritants?" (in the *First-Rate First Dates: Increasing the Chances of a Second Date* book) I discussed the timing of the telling. If you decide to say something, timing, word choice and tone are important.

We also need to examine how trainable we are. How do you respond when your date asks you to change something?

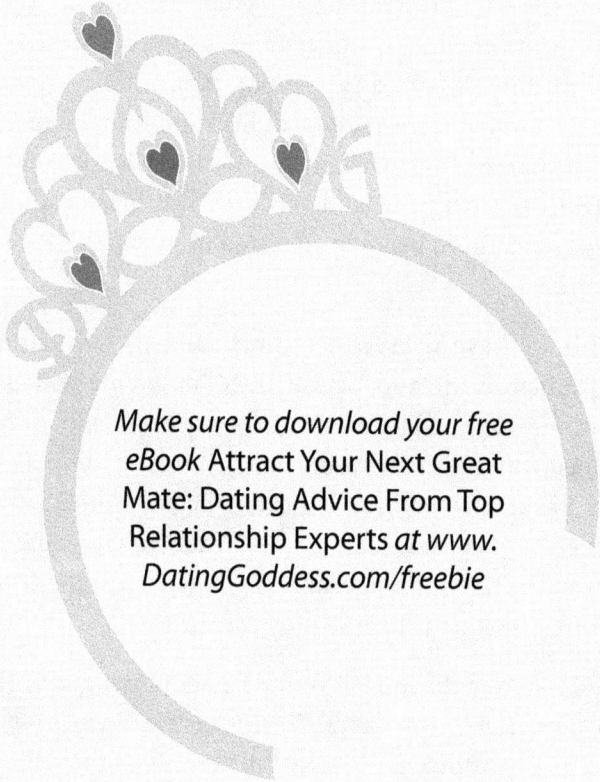

Make sure to download your free eBook *Attract Your Next Great Mate: Dating Advice From Top Relationship Experts* at www. DatingGoddess.com/freebie

Do you treat him like a friend?

"Love and friendship exclude each other."
—Jean de la Bruyere

Common wisdom is that long-term relationships are based on solid friendship. I agree. But I do ponder where is the line between how you'd treat a friend and how you treat your beau.

For example, with my very best friends I can talk about anything. Yes, anything. My fears, doubts, insecurities. I can boast about a recent success and they won't think less of me. I can vent about some recent interaction. I can share my hopes for the future.

I'd hope I can say these things to a long-term partner, too. The challenge comes with knowing the line — if there is a line — of what to share and what not.

For example, if a friend is considering doing something I think is ill-advised, I feel I have the right, and in the cases of very good friends, the responsibility, to say something. Some less-than-good friends would say, "Butt out. It's none of your business." But I expect my friends to point out if they think I'm overlooking something important. In other words, if they think I'm about to do — or maybe even in the middle of doing — something stupid, they speak up.

Luckily, my friends are socially adept and don't blurt out "You're being stupid," or "Don't you have a brain in your head?" or "What could you possibly be thinking?" These phrases are more likely to come from family, not friends.

But I've been unsuccessful, no matter how gently I think I've phrased it, to suggest to a beau that his course of action may benefit from some additional thinking. No. When I've tried this a few times, I sometimes hear that I'm treating him like a child.

Some say to just let him do what he planned and fall on his face

So what to do? Some say to just let him do what he planned and fall on his face. Or live with the consequences. Or maybe it will pan out to his satisfaction, even though you know it would be even better with your added input. I know, this sounds arrogant. But the beauty of two heads is they often are really better than one, and better solutions are created by melding two good minds.

Could you watch a friend do something you think

— perhaps know — is dumb, without saying something? Would you stand by if a friend was going to dive off a bridge into what seemed like a deep pond without first checking if there were big rocks under the surface that could crack her head? What if she got excited about joining a new multi-level marketing venture and decided to quit her job, even though she was sole support of herself and her two kids? What if she decided to go to Vegas this weekend to marry that man she's known only four weeks? Could you not at least discuss it with her or him?

A friend long ago counseled me that men don't want their sweetie's input. They want to be successful without any of her suggestions. They can feel emasculated if she contributes ideas he didn't think of. My friend said to just let my ex do what he would do and praise him whatever the result. Now talk about infantilizing! This seems like something you'd do to a small child.

Perhaps I'm naive, but I envision my mate being someone who asks for and welcomes my input on his plans. Not everything, of course, but big issues. I often seek others' input — including those I'm dating. I'm not put off by their ideas, even if I've thought of them all before. I appreciate their willingness to noodle on the situation with me. And I welcome someone's suggesting there might be issues they want to make sure I've considered. To me, this is a way they show they care. As long as they do it without the aforementioned condescension.

The rub happens when there is no request for help

from the other, if you just jump in unasked. With good friends, I think there is an implicit — and sometimes explicit — permission to jump in anytime you see something you think would be useful to the other. My more evolved friends have a standard practice of asking, "Do you want my input?" or "Would you like to brainstorm this?" or "Would you like some more ideas on how to accomplish what you want?"

I always say yes when asked, and have yet to be refused when I've asked this of my friends. So what is the big deal when it comes to someone in which you're having a romantic relationship? You're friends as well as dating, right? So why can't you treat him the same way you treat your good friends?

Share your perspective on this issue. Do you find you can treat a beau as you would your friends? Or are there some areas that are verboten?

Do his fingers hold clues to his behavior?

Hold your hands in front of you. Notice if your ring finger is longer than your index (pointing) finger. Are they the same size? If so, or if your ring finger is shorter, you're a typical woman. If the ring finger is longer, you're atypical.

Ask your next date to do this test. The size of a man's, er, digits, may tell you a lot.

"Who cares? you say. "Is this a silly parlor game?"

In a "Salon" article called "Cupid's Science," reporter Rebecca Traister interviewed Chemistry.com creator, anthropologist Helen Fisher, Ph.D. Dr. Fisher is also the author of *Why We Love: The Nature and Chemistry of Romantic Love* and *Anatomy of Love: The Natural History of Mating, Marriage,* and *Why We Stray*. In a discussion about the site's profile assessment and one unusual question, she divulged a little-known fact: your fingers can speak volumes.

No, not just that one digit you raise in anger.

But your index and ring fingers. At least their ratio to each other's length.

Dr. Fisher explains that "digit ratio" is related to the estrogen/testosterone ratio that begins before birth.

"In the womb, the brain is washed over by estrogen and testosterone. If you have a lot more testosterone than estrogen in the womb, it is going to build a longer fourth finger than second finger. If you've got a lot more estrogen in the womb, the pointer finger will be longer.

Not just that one digit you raise in anger.

"There are three testosterone bursts: one in the womb, one in infancy and a giant spurt in puberty. But if you have more testosterone in the womb and you have a longer fourth finger, you're more likely to have musical ability, mathematical abilities, to be an engineer or architect or good at computer programming. You tend to have poorer social skills but be direct, decisive, ambitious, competitive. What they call 'extreme male brain' is when you're overly flooded with testosterone and are pushed into the autistic spectrum. And football players are very high on testosterone and estrogen.

So you can be high in both.

"[If you have more estrogen, you usually] have good verbal skills, can find the right word rapidly, are good at remembering, better at compassion, nurturing, patience, have good people skills, and are better at reading posture, gesture, tone of voice and facial features."

Now I'm not here to argue if male/female stereotypes are, in fact, based on science, or that one can be decisive, direct, competitive and ambitious even with a puny ring finger. These are mostly skills that can be learned, just as can compassion, memory, verbal and people skills. She's talking about natural inclinations, not learned skills here.

So experiment with this one. Notice the finger ratio on your next date. Then see he fits Dr. Fisher's findings or if he has great people skills despite his handicap of a longer ring finger. Report back to us what you find.

(BTW, my ring finger is slightly longer.)

The importance of
sweet talk

Y ou've developed a fondness for each other in several long phone conversations, so you agree to meet. There are signs he's attracted — he touches you gently, holds your hand, looks you in the eye, pays attention to what you say, asks about you and your interests, seems interested in pleasing you.

You are drawn to him, too. Yet something seems missing. What?

You'd like some verbal confirmation. Guys might say "What are you talking about? The guy's showing he's interested!" But it's nice to hear it, too.

Something seems missing. What?

I like it when a guy compliments me, says he's glad to see me, that I look nice, smell good, etc. It reassures me. Of course, he could be using his usual, "You are beautiful" line that he says to every woman, but it still sounds good to me!

I also like it when he uses endearing terms: "sweetheart," "darling," "my dear," "babe," "sugar," even "sweetie" will do. Hey, I'll even take "sugar cookie," "snookums," "cupcake," "blueberry muffin," or "my sweet baboo" (yes, I've been called all those). Some even call me "goddess," which of course I adore! (Please — no "poopsie!)

While sometimes talk can be cheap, often it is worth millions. A few endearing comments can melt my heart and has occasionally made me more enamored with a guy than I might have without them.

So when you like something about a guy, let him know. If you feel a fondness, let a "sweetie" slip out. It might — or might not — mean as much to him, but if he's astute he will hear what you like and return it in kind.

But don't overdo it. Many feel too many "sweeties" on the first date shows too much assumptive closeness too soon.

I have been told by a guy pal that when a man can't remember your name on a date, he calls you "sweetie." You think it's endearing; he gets off the hook.

Does your date nourish your mind?

My friend bestselling author Mark Sanborn wrote an recent article about relationships. "Some of my best relationships … challenge me intellectually and spiritually. Scott Peck believed that love was about the commitment to another's growth, and that makes sense to me."

I agree! I find potential suitors' conversations uninteresting that mostly discuss the weather. If I try to take the conversation deeper and he doesn't want to go there, that is a good sign this guy isn't for me. I can give him grace if he says he's tired and doesn't want to think that hard, but if he doesn't ever want to discuss anything thought provoking, I'm not willing to spend my time that way.

During the 2.5 hour drive with the golf addict (see see the *Ironing Out Dating Wrinkles: Work Through Challenges Without Getting Steamed* book), he continually complained about the traffic. Since there was nothing we could do about the traffic, I said, "Let's play a game. My mastermind group did this interesting exercise. We each listed 5 books, CDs and DVDs that we'd want to have if we were stranded on a desert island — with enough batteries to keep the DVD/CD player going. What would be some of your choices?" He said he didn't want to think that hard.

This wasn't the first (nor last) time he'd avoided a conversation that required more than "reporting" (weather, work, etc.).

I love it when I can discuss topics that get me to think and perhaps change my perspective. I don't like obnoxious, in-your-face discussions, but ones that are sane and rational and you can be heard without being treated like you're an idiot for thinking a certain way. And I like hearing perspectives that are different than my own.

However, some people don't look for that in a date. They just want to have a good time, which for some, apparently means talking about things that I find uninteresting and unimportant. Of course, there is always a certain amount of "How was your day?" kind of conversation in

I love it when I can discuss topics that get me to think

any close relationship. But if that is the main course of conversation, it is like subsisting on only sugar. It is mind-numbing when your body really wants — per-

haps craves — more nutritious nourishment.

And what about Scott Peck's belief that love is about the commitment to another's growth? Do you believe that? I do. I want my partner to help me grow and I want a partner who is open to my encouraging and supporting him to grow. That doesn't mean we nag each other when we see a habit we don't like. It means we share what we want to work on and tell the other how s/he can support us in making changes. It also means s/he celebrates with us when we make those changes or experience growth.

What's your expectation about your guy and growth?

Is he willing to be vulnerable?

Women typically say they want a guy who is willing to be vulnerable with them, and with whom they can be the same. I've dated some men for months who never shared a vulnerable thought, even if I asked about his hopes, fears, dreams and regrets. Nothing.

So I was pleased that a man I've been talking to for 3 weeks, but we haven't yet met, was comfortable enough to cry on the phone with me. The circumstances were extenuating: his mother had just died, it was the day before the funeral, none of his siblings would help with the funeral in any way so everything fell on him. He was stressed over this, grief stricken, getting pressure from his job to return to work. Anyone would have cracked at this — or even less.

I was glad he comfortable enough to cry with me

He didn't seem to be embarrassed, nor did he apologize as some men do when they show emotion. Men are typically socialized to not share their sadness, and heaven forbid they cry. "Only sissies cry" seems to be branded into many men's psyche.

In "Is he a 'soft place to fall'?" (page 91) I talked about how important it is for most women to have a man with whom they can be vulnerable. But the reverse is true for some men, too, even if they aren't a "Sensitive, New Age Guy." And just like he doesn't want someone who is so emotionally unstable that you blubber at the sign of a dead flower, so, too, you don't want a guy who seems to be taking estrogen injections.

How do you feel about men who are willing to show their emotions? Is there a length of time you feel you need to know each other before being that emotionally honest?

146

Do you let hunky men get away with more?

You may answer, "No. A man has to treat me right or he's out of my life, no matter how handsome he is."

Or perhaps you realize that good looks do buy some good will, often more than is warranted. It isn't something most of us are proud to admit, but yes, we do allow hunky men to get by with some behaviors we wouldn't accept from others. Shallow, I know.

During my 5-month whirlwind romance with a handsome and chiseled man, a good friend repeatedly asked, "Would you put up with his nonsense if he wasn't so good looking?" I sheepishly answered, "Probably not."

Part of it, I think, is we consider the whole package when we make our decisions about what to tolerate and when to put our foot down. If my ex-beau had been only eye candy, the tolerance threshold would have been much lower. I've gone out with handsome men who were arrogant, selfish, and inarticulate, all of which are turn offs. So if a man is only great looking, there's not enough to hold my interest. But if exceptional looks are coupled with other attractive characteristics, the combination can cause you to look the other way when faced with marginally acceptable behaviors.

I've often said, "Yummy is as yummy does" since an average-looking man becomes more attractive as you get to know his kind, generous, romantic or courageous spirit. And I'm not proud to admit that sometimes yummy does provide indulgences for not-so-yummy behaviors.

Yummy does provide indulgences for not-so-yummy behaviors.

So should you not date hot men? You should date anyone you find interesting, stimulating, and attractive. But be vigilant in noticing what you accept that you wouldn't endure in a not-so-handsome man. You should be treated always with the utmost respect and not lower your standards just because he's gorgeous.

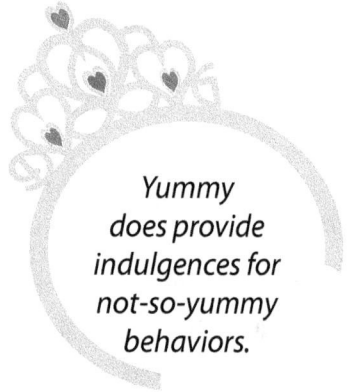

Where have all the good men gone?

Just as the song "Where Have All the Flowers Gone" mourns the disappearance of things that are important to us, my gal pal bewailed her experience not finding interesting eligible bachelors. She said, "Where are the dynamic men — like me? Where are the funny men — like me? Where are the adventurous men — like me? Where are the intelligent men — like me?"

Although she is 6 weeks shy of her 50th birthday, her last few beaus have been in their twenties. Men she encountered her own age were unable to keep up with her energetic activities, were stuck in their ways, or had children in tow. She was an entrepreneurial free spirit, spending much of the last year abroad. She wanted someone who would match her zest, curiosity and positive outlook on life. They were not showing up on Match.com.

I joined her lament, as few of the men I've met in this adventure have had many of the elements she and I both sought. Although I have met some wonderful treasures, so far no one who I thought was "The One," although a few had many of the characteristics I was seeking.

My friend decided to join some new online sites focused on her values. She was advised to hang out where like minds congregated. So she's attending seminars where she hopes to not only get inspiration and information, but to meet an evenly matched man.

Her tactic is not a new one. It is common advice to attend events and classes where others of similar interests convene. This way you'll at least enjoy the activity, whether or not you find romance. Of course, if you only like quilting, fashion shows and flower arranging, it will be harder to find a man, although some men do enjoy such activities.

I believe you will find your love match when the time is right. And yes, you have to be out in the world in order to do so. But I don't think you should necessarily make a point of hanging out in the hardware store, computer shop or monster truck rally to find a guy, unless you like those places anyway.

So, have faith, do what you love to do outside the house, and put a smile on your face. And remember that he's looking for you, too!

You treat yourself as you were treated

After my latest breakup, I decided to get to the bottom of why I would stay in a relationship that wasn't meeting my needs and put up with behaviors I wouldn't accept from a friend, let alone a beau. I've engaged the help of a psychologist friend, Ben, to help me root out the cause and heal whatever allowed me to stay in a relationship that a part of me knew was not good for me.

In our first session, as I was beating myself up for ignoring the red flags that were all but slapping me in the face, he said, "Let me share with you Psychology 101: You treat yourself as you were treated." In other words, if you were treated with belittlement and put downs, your inner dialog is also hypercritical and judgmental of you. It's been ingrained in you since you were little and you don't even know that voice is there much of the time.

And how you were treated is how you would expect others — especially a potential mate — would treat you. If you grew up in an environment where your wishes were ignored, your needs seldom met, or behaviors didn't match words, you would be attracted to someone who says he cares deeply about you, yet makes just the minimum effort to satisfy you. Just enough so you have hope he will give you more.

The key to attracting someone who will treat you well is to treat yourself well. I know, this sounds overly simplistic, but bear with me.

If you internally think you aren't worthy of love since your parents didn't show you love in a way that felt like love to you, you'll attract a man who will not treat you in a way that feels loving. That is not to say he or they didn't/don't love you — but they express it their way, which may not feel like love to you.

> The key to attracting someone who will treat you well is to treat yourself well

For example, my mother gave me a baby doll for my fourteenth birthday. I was never much into baby dolls and hadn't played with dolls in many years. Yet she liked dolls, and she thought this one was pretty, so she bought it for me. She felt she was doing something loving by buying me something she thought was nice. I, however, saw this as tangible evidence she had no idea who I was nor what I liked. I see now it was her way of expressing love, but that was not how it felt to me at the time.

The key, Ben says, is to reprogram that inner tape to give you the messages that are empowering, not the negative ones that will perpetuate the pattern that doesn't work for you. I know, I know, this sounds so common sense — and one would think that just because it is so logical and simple to understand it is easy to apply. Have you ever tried reprogramming deep-seated inner messages? It is far from easy.

By talking out with Ben the messages that made me attract, enter into and hang onto a relationship that didn't my needs, I am more conscious of them. If I'm aware of the inner dialog that makes me believe in, then behave in ways that are counter to my needs getting met, I have more control over changing the messages as well as the dysfunctional behaviors.

What deep-seated messages do you know run through your brain that keep you repeating unhealthy behaviors? If you've been successful modifying them, what has worked for you?

Can he afford you?

hile in Dubai, I befriended a 28-year-old local professional man who shared the romantic reality for many like him. His description made me think of some parallels to Western dating, although, of course, there are huge differences.

He explained that men and women are commonly match-made through their families. The women often require a groom's dowry. For example, a woman wants her husband to provide her with the same standard of living that her father provides her, even though her father is well established financially and her intended husband is just starting out.

So she expects him to provide her the same level of designer clothing, upscale housing, exclusive club memberships, exotic vacations, and regular spa visits.

Then there's the one-up game. If her sister's husband bought her a Lexus then she insists on a Mercedes. If her sister got a 3-bedroom house, she wants a 4-bedroom.

So before he asks or agrees to marry her, the man decides if he can afford her. Can he keep up with her (and her parent's) demands?

In dating, part of deciding if you are a match is not only discovering if you have similar values, interests and sensibilities, but also similar economic expectations. It is common for midlife couples to have somewhat equal incomes, or the man to make more. It has become more commonplace for the woman to earn more. But for all the advancements toward equality, there is still a prevalent expectation that the man will buy most of the dating dinners and some other expenses during the wooing process, or they will take turns treating.

If the man can't afford to at least pay half, it can sour the relationship no matter how much a woman is into him. He can be the sweetest, kindest, most loving man and yet if he can't afford a similar lifestyle, it is a short-lived relationship. One or both of them can't tolerate the imbalance.

I've experienced this myself. While I can be drawn to a man for his great personality, economics do enter into my decision whether to continue to see him or not. I feel shallow to admit it, but it is true. I think, in part, it's because I was married to a financially strapped man for 20 years and felt it put restraints on what we were able to do. I paid more than my share of many things and supplemented vacations and home improvements. At the time I said it didn't really matter but the truth is it began to stick in my craw. I felt like I was carrying a man who was unwilling to step up and at least shoulder his own weight.

So while economics can seem superficial, it affects activities and lifestyle. If you want to have exotic vacations and he can't afford to pay his way, you can foot the bill. If you enjoy 5-star restaurants and he can only spring for diners, you can treat. But for most couples, it will eventually cause a rift. Even if you have a high unending stream of income, you can begin to feel taken advantage of.

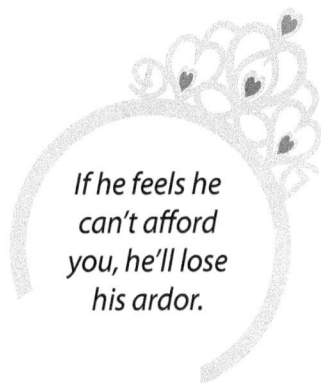

> *If he feels he can't afford you, he'll lose his ardor.*

And if he feels he can't afford you, he will lose his ardor. A man needs to believe he can make his woman happy and if he feels her needs are beyond his capabilities or interest, he'll cut her lose. One date admitted his last relationship ended because she wanted to "live life large" with a big house, fancy car, and foreign vacations. And while she made a good income, it wasn't enough to support that lifestyle for both of them. He said at his age — mid fifties — he really didn't want to work that hard to make that kind of money. He wanted to spend more time with his kids and on his hobbies than at work earning money to support a lifestyle he didn't really want. So he broke up with his girlfriend since it was clear they had different life goals and values.

Have you begun to date someone who you really

liked, but you realized you had different lifestyle expec-tations? Did you decide to continue seeing him or pull the plug when you saw your economic dreams looked different?

My gay "boyfriend"

He sent a beautiful bouquet for my birthday last month, arranging for its arrival the day I returned home from SE Asia. He's accompanied me to dress-up events, donning his Armani tuxedo with pleasure. He's the epitome of a gentleman at these events, offering his arm to escort me, taking my coat and fetching it from the coat check, holding my chair to seat me, making sure my drink is never low, dancing when I want and schmoozing with my business associates, even ones I know he doesn't like. He keeps himself buff, is current on world affairs, is respected as a thought leader, is generous with charitable contributions.

So why isn't he my full time beau?

He's gay. Not bisexual.

Drat!

The other day another gay friend asked if I'd ever fallen for a gay man thinking he was straight. Yes, in high school my regular "beau" for two years was an attentive, well-dressed, fun guy who came out after going off to college. I can't say I was surprised as we never shared more than a peck kiss, but he was so much of what I wanted in a boyfriend I overlooked the obvious signs that everyone else gladly pointed out to me.

I asked my friend why he asked the question. He said a lot of women fall for gay men because they are often so much of what the women want. There are exceptions, of course, but the gay men I know tend to be well groomed, take care of their bodies, are considerate, com-

> *A lot of women fall for gay men because they are often so much of what the women want.*

municative, affectionate, smart, accomplished, witty and funny. What's not to fall for? In fact, some women think they would make the perfect boyfriend if you're not interested in sex. The women say they would look the other way while he gets his physical needs met and she gets her emotional, social, intellectual and some physical needs met, like cuddling.

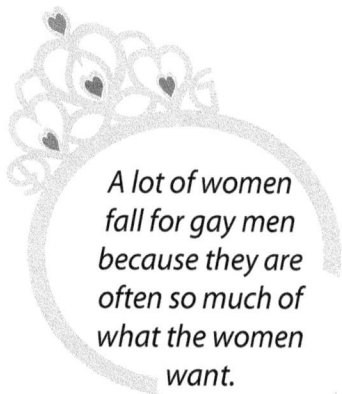

While I'm very fond of my gay "boyfriend" I'm not delusional that it is anything but friendship that he's expressing. The movie "The Object of My Affection" portrays the situation where Nina (Jennifer Aniston) falls for her friend George (Paul Rudd) fully knowing he's gay. He is everything her jerk ex-boyfriend is not: communicative, affectionate, able to express his caring for her, nurturing and cooperative. He moves in with her after his boyfriend breaks up with him. Watching them take dance lessons you see the chemistry between them. But her heart breaks when she has to confront the fact that she has fallen in love with a man who can never love her the way she wants to be loved.

So if you have men in your life who you know aren't available to you, make sure you keep your wits about you and don't read into their thoughtful behaviors as more than friendship. Just appreciate who they are and love them like a brother.

Wanted: A man with a plan

In *1*, Steve Harvey says if a man doesn't have a plan you should not fall for him.

A "plan" means a vision for his future and how he will get there. That plan needs to include a woman in it. I've been surprised that some men have a plan for themselves, but it doesn't seem to include a woman. For example, a wealthy man I dated several times had already planned his retirement by buying a small, 2-bedroom condo hundreds of miles away to which he will move when he retires in a few years. He remodeled and furnished it how he likes it.

I admired that he was so proactive and had a clear plan. But what would he do about integrating a woman into this plan? I envisioned that if it worked out between us I'd have to buy the condo next door for me and my stuff! Or sell all my belongings, I guess. In our many hours of phone conversations, there was never any mention of, "This is my plan if I'm alone. If and when I am partnered again, we'd figure out a new plan together."

At the other end of the spectrum are the men (yes, more than one) who have fully integrated me into their lives — often before even meeting me. They have pictured me moving into their home and accompanying them through the lives they've established. I even had one ask if I'd take his last name after we were married! It always astonished me that these men wanted me to slide into their lives and activities without any mention of how they would integrate into my life. It was as if they were acquiring a new pet.

All in all, though, I appreciate a man with a plan for his life — one that includes the possibility of a woman helping to determine some parts of that future together. It is important to know if a man's plan is to retire to some remote area to fish and watch sports. That holds no interest for me, so no matter how much I like him, if that is all he envisions, he's not the one for me.

Of course, it's important for you to have a vision and plan for your future, otherwise you could be swept up in whatever plan your man had for himself, and that may or may not make you happy. Some women without a plan awaken after a few years to discover they are unhappy with their life because they didn't give much thought to their own plan.

The man's plan has to include how he plans to court you, if he decides he wants you. He can't just be "kickin'" with you, unless that's what you want, too. If you want someone to build a future with in a committed relationship, you could "kick" with him for years then find out he has no interest in being committed to anyone. So best to find out his plans about his life and relationships near the beginning.

A man has come back into my life after a year abroad. He admitted to me that while he has dreams, he takes one day at a time. Unfortunately, that means he isn't taking the steps needed to make his dreams become reality. Because of this lackadaisical attitude, I have no long-term interest in him.

How do you feel about a man with vs. without a plan? Would you date someone for long who didn't have a plan for his life and how you might fit in it?

DatingGoddess.com

Command presence

For decades (centuries?) women have been drawn to men in uniform. Is it the crispness of their attire that is the allure? The fact that you know they've learned responsibility and discipline from being in the service? Some appeal to our desire for a man who knows how to protect us? The respect we have for the sacrifice we know the wearer has and is willing to make?

My stay back in Brunei this week overlaps a large SE Asia military convention and air show. My hotel and the city are filled with military men and women. At the main shopping mall, I observed dozens of mostly men from all ranks in their country's uniform.

While not all the men have a draw, I notice some do. In fact, I saw some Americans who were not in uniform, but had a certain bearing that makes me believe they are either in or have been in the military.

I've decided that a big part of a man in uniform's appeal, whether he's from the military or other military-based organizations like fire or police, is their carriage and posture. I'm told it's called "command presence."

When I dated a retired policeman, he said he'd

167

learned how to stand and walk in a way that people knew he was in charge. He shared that this deportment could quell a brewing problem as those involved could tell by his stance that he was not going to take any gruff. His posture telegraphed confidence.

Of course, not all those in uniform carry themselves with gravitas. But those who do have a certain je ne sais quoi enticement. I've noticed a man who is not classically handsome can be quite enticing if his carriage is confident.

What have you noticed about a man's posture and bearing and how it affects your attraction to him?

The wallet triage

In past postings we have talked about dating's financial conundrums and how to find balance. We've discussed how different financial values and capabilities cause conflict.

In dating, whether we realize it or not, we begin to do what was called a "wallet triage" by one of my hospital clients. This distasteful term was used to describe when they had to determine if a patient could pay for treatment. If not, they had to be sent to the county hospital. It was unpleasant for the staff to ask the uncomfortable questions about someone's ability to pay while the patient was bleeding or in pain, and it was distressing for those being asked. But the hospital was hemorrhaging funds, and if they treated people without receiving payment, the hospital was going to close, which would have put the community in dire straights. It was a horrible situation for all concerned.

The dating wallet triage is determining if someone's financial situation is something with which you can live. Especially if the other is in dire straights because of their decisions, not only because of the recession.

This week, a wooer disclosed that he owed the IRS tens of thousands of dollars in back taxes and penalties, plus some other debts. The government recently took ALL the money from his accounts. (Luckily, he was not asking me for any.)

Another man recently shared that he, too, owes back taxes and the IRS now garnishes any funds deposited to his accounts. He goes to check cashing outlets to cash his clients' checks to get money for gas, food, etc.

I know these times are hard for many, many people. Both these men are intelligent professionals who made some unwise decisions that have caught up with them. I, too, have had financial ups and downs so I empathize with them both.

But as I ponder entering a relationship with a new man, I know I want someone who is financially sound. He doesn't have to be weathly, but he needs to have his life mostly in order.

Both these men are natty dressers. The first one recently took a week-long vacation and shared he'd bought some new shoes, since he's a shoe fancier. I don't know about you, but if I have a closet full of functional shoes and owe the government tens of thousands of dollars, I'm not going to buy any new shoes, no matter how much I like them.

My ex floated a large debt for nearly all of our marriage. I have been in debt, and when I am, I don't buy anything extraneous. I live frugally and put all my extra funds toward paying off that debt in months instead of years. My ex saw no problem with buying frivolous items even though he had large debt. It's a matter of different values and priorities. I hate to be in debt and do everything I can to avoid it, and if I can't, I pay it off quickly.

I found that being with a man who was always in debt meant we couldn't do things that were important to me — and he said were important to him, too — or I would pay for them all myself. So when it was time to paint the house, he didn't have the money (we'd usually split these expenses), so I paid for it. I didn't mind paying for vacations or household improvements sometimes. But I resented it when he said he didn't have the money to do what we both said was needed, then would buy something frivolous for himself.

You have to look at your own values around money and what's important to you. If a man shows early on his values about money are very different than yours, best to discuss it if you can, or let him go. If his situation is temporary because of the recession, that's one thing. But if he continues to make what you consider unwise decisions, best to move on as you'll be fighting about money sooner or later.

"You're more valuable than a wife"

After several months of daily conversations and a few in-person dates, this out-of-state suitor shared his sentiment. I felt complimented, but at the same time quizzical.

I appreciated that he frequently sought and took my business counsel. But it made me think that he didn't value a wife very highly. It stalled my desire to take our relationship to the next level. If it weren't for my business acumen, would he respect me? Would he only engage my opinion if it were business related, and not about other aspects of our relationship?

So what would happen in the future when he retires and no longer needs a live-in savvy business advisor? What role would he relegate to his wife (possibly me)? Would she (I?) be consigned traditional roles of cooking, cleaning, household aesthetics and matrimonial duties? Would she/I be required to look good, keep up the house, but say nothing of consequence?

He said he is cautious about making more romantic advances as he's afraid he'd lose me as his treasured advisor. Which is actually fine with me as I want a man who is looking for a full-fledged partner, not a mentor with benefits.

When my ex and I met, we were in the same profession but my career was much more established than his, despite him being 14 years older. He'd switched careers shortly before we met. Throughout our 20-year marriage, he'd ask my advice and rarely took it. I'd see him struggle with tasks that I could show him how to accomplish easily. But I learned to keep my mouth shut. In the end, he said that my competency in so many areas made him feel emasculated, even though he said I never rubbed it in his face.

So I am loathe to take on a romantic relationship again with someone who needs my business savvy. It could work to be in business together or help each other, but only if we were at the same level and we were adding our perspective and expertise to the other.

Have you felt that someone you were dating valued you more as an advisor and wanted romance? What did you find were the pros/cons?

I'm in love

He's tall — 6'3-1/2".

He's dark — with a perpetual tan.

He's handsome — drop dead gorgeous.

He has a deep, sexy voice.

He's funny, humble and adorable.

He's athletic — a former NFL player.

Our 19-year age difference doesn't seem to matter.

There's only one problem…

We've never met.

In fact, he has no idea I'm alive.

And there's that pesky issue of his girlfriend.

Plus, I'm afraid I'm not the only woman who has gone gaga for this man. In fact, not just straight women are entranced. Ellen DeGeneres said she had to meet him once she saw him.

So I guess there's more than one problem.

In case you haven't figured it out yet, my love interest is an actor. But not the usual George, Brad or Colin.

He's Isaiah Mustafa, "the man your man could smell like" in the 2010 Old Spice commercials.

While we women know that there are few midlife men who have Isaiah's all-over charm and stunning good looks, we can always admire those god-like specimens from afar. As long as we don't reject the mere mortals who have other stellar qualities coupled with perhaps a little paunch, receding hairline, or wrinkles. Just as we hope they accept that unlike Jen, Angelina and Halle, we have crow's feet, muffin tops, and cellulite.

We can pay tribute to modern day Narcissus's and Aphrodites, but more often the true gods and goddesses come in less striking packages. Their divineness exudes through their kindness, compassion, caring and generosity.

What intelligences do
you possess?

The doctor in my exercise class is always off a beat. He enthusiastically flails his arms and legs — if occasionally in time with music it is by mere accident. I wonder how it would be to be coupled with a highly intelligent man who had no rhythm and no consciousness that his body is moving very differently than our instructor.

We all have an idea of our perfect mate. Perhaps he's artistic, articulate, rational, a great dancer, musically adept, introspective, appreciative of nature, and a great communicator.

If you want all of the above, good luck. As they represent competency in each of the 8 intelligences Harold Gardner presented in his 1983 theory on multiple intelligences.

Spatial

Linguistic

Logical-mathematical

Kinesthetic

Musical

Interpersonal

Intrapersonal

Naturalist

You say, "But the description above is just of well-rounded person. Nothing really grandiose." Perhaps. It depends on the level of proficiency you desire in each of the intelligences. If you want someone with a 10 in each, you are living in a fantasy.

Most of us have one dominant intelligence, according to Gardner's hypothesis. Or perhaps two. You may be average at a few. And one or more that just aren't a strength.

Take a stab at rating yourself on a 1-10 scale on each of the intelligences listed above. If you are a concert pianist, you would be a 10 in the musical intelligence. A Ph.D. in mathematics, no doubt a 10 in logical/mathematical. An architect — spatial. (More examples at <u>Wikipedia.</u>)

For example, I'd give myself an 8 or 9 for linguistic since I'm a writer and speaker. I'd give myself a 6 at kinesthetic since I'm a reasonable dancer, but would never qualify for "So You Think You Can Dance."

After you've subjectively rated yourself, now rate your ideal mate in these 8 areas. If you're an 8 on kinesthetic, would you be willing to couple with a 3? If you're a 4 in logical/mathematical would you see yourself with a 9?

Of course, you can fall in love with someone who has polar opposite natural skill sets. In fact, some schools teach to all 8 intelligences to get kids to improve their appreciation of each, and perhaps their skill level. So if you have two left feet, will you ever be an exceptional dancer? Probably not. But if you continue to develop your skills you will at least be better — and your 8-level kinesthetic partner will enjoy your dance outings even more.

Appreciate not only your various intelligences as well as your date's. However, know which ones you require and which ones you can live with if he's not as good as you.

But if your partner insists that you engage in activities that come naturally to him and are hard and thus not enjoyable to you, best to communicate that you won't be joining him in that activity. If he insists, that's a sign it's time to put your foot down — or out the door.

Hunkalicious

Bulging biceps. Chiseled pecs. Taut tushes.

The gym is part of their daily regimen.

They look great in — or out of — their clothes.

I describe these guys as "hunkalicious."

Sometimes the only muscles they've developed are below the neck. Holding an extended conversation about anything of intellectual value is a challenge.

But sometimes they have the whole package. Buff and brainy. Fit and funny. Athletic and articulate.

This was the description of #103 who I met a few days ago. He is a refreshing mix of uncommon characteristics. I was initially drawn to him because of his online pictures, and his profile revealed a well-spoken man. I was pleased that the man in person was thoughtful, respectful and easy going.

I, too, have stereotyped buff men. I've thought they wouldn't be interested in me because I'm not buff and wouldn't want to spend a lot of time in the gym, although I do exercise.

I'm actually glad to find out I'm wrong in those assumptions.

What assumptions have you made about men's values, priorities and intellectual capacity based on their rippling muscles?

Handsome men who don't know it

Good-looking men are nearly always alluring. Some ruin it, however, when you spend time with them. Their good looks have made them arrogant, vain, insensitive and/or jerks. They are used to women treating them well even if they behave badly.

In an episode of "30 Rock" Jon Hamm played a handsome doctor who Tina Fey's character described as living in a bubble. People bent over backwards for him, but he thought that was how all people were treated. He had no idea that the generosity he experienced wasn't commonplace.

Other men use their good looks to manipulate others. Some are con artists, exemplified memorably by Brad Pitt's character in "Thelma and Louise." Not only did he seduce Geena Davis' character, but he took all her money afterward.

So it's refreshing when a good-looking man doesn't know he is. He's not so stunningly gorgeous that women throw themselves after him. But he's handsome enough that you are happy to be seen on his arm.

I had a few dates recently with a man who was incredulous when I told him he was handsome. I don't think it was false modesty, but he didn't have the experience of women fawning over him. His humility, of course, increased his attractiveness.

Handsome men who don't know it are the best beaus. You don't have to pretend you find him attractive, yet if he doesn't see himself through your eyes he's appreciative of your perspective. Instead of taking your compliments for granted, "Yes, I am good looking," he humbly thanks you.

Men underestimate women's need to feel safe

We'd talked on the phone a few times but hadn't met. It was early evening when we talked again and he said he'd love to take me to dinner that night. But he had a favor to ask: his Jag was in the shop so would I drive to his area for dinner?

He lived 45 minutes away in a newly gentrified part of a not-so-great area. It was already dark. I didn't relish driving to his area after sunset.

When I said that, he scoffed, trying to cajole me. I wouldn't budge. "I'm not driving there alone after dark." He said he lived in a safe part of town. "But," I responded, "I have to drive through a not-so-safe part to get to your part." He got exasperated.

This wasn't the first time a man had disregarded my concern for my safety. I hadn't been able to articulate this before I listened to a recording from a seminar about men and women. The seminar leader asked how many men had been cognizant of their personal safety in the last month. No men's hands raised. She then asked the women. Every hand raised.

In dating, women need to be conscious about creating safe environments for themselves. This is why we are advised to always meet a man in a public place for the first few dates, and to always drive in your own car until you've vetted the man. I've ignored this advice a few times and while nothing happened, it could have. In retrospect, I saw how stupid I was and how lucky I was that nothing happened.

We don't want to be paranoid, yet if you are a trusting person, you give men that trust before they have earned it. I don't even like a man to pick me up at my house on the second date. I've found too many see that as an invitation to more than I'd wanted.

Since many men don't understand that they need to make sure the woman feels safe, look for the signs of his insensitivity. If while planning a date he chides you for insisting you drive yourself to the rendezvous site, he's not the kind of conscientious man you want. If he tries to persuade you that he will "be good" or "a gentleman" when you say you're not comfortable going to his house for a second-date dinner, he's trying to manipulate you.

Be clear on what you need to feel safe. Think about it ahead of time so you can express yourself confidently and firmly. If he tries to negotiate what you state you need to feel comfortable, he'll try to press your boundaries until he gets his way.

You don't want to be paranoid, but few women have been sorry they've erred on the side of caution. The women who are regretful are the ones who ignored their inner voice screaming "this doesn't feel comfortable" then allowing the man to lead them where they didn't want to go.

You always want to be equipped to get yourself out of a situation that becomes uncomfortable. The challenge is that you may feel comfortable with a man on the first few dates so agree to things you know could be risky. You probably don't know the man very well as you start dating. So he could be perfectly nice in public on the first few dates. But behind closed doors he could show a side that makes you uncomfortable. This is why it's important to keep your dates to public places for a while. If he has controlling tendencies, they will begin to leak out soon enough.

Have you experienced men who try to convince you that your cautiousness is unfounded? How did you respond? Have you found yourself in situations that you realize could have ended badly? Any experiences that started innocently but caused you to extricate yourself because you didn't feel safe?

The joy of boy toys

Younger men. Sometimes decades younger. Perhaps young enough to be your son.

I'm not usually drawn to them because they are typically even more immature than the fifty-somethings I tend to date. And I abhor the concept of and term "cougar" so would never want to be accused of one.

But every once in a while a younger man comes along who is worth considering. And if there's mutual attraction, it can be great for your ego — as well as fun!

A few months ago I had a few dates and continue to be contact with one such man. He is more emotionally mature than many of the chronologically mature men with whom I've gone out, despite his being 20 years my junior. He's handsome, interesting, thoughtful, intelligent — and he thinks I'm sexy and, in his words, "gorgeous." I usually only get that from the near-sighted men closer to my own age.

Yesterday a 40-year-old colleague called and the topic turned to his 63-year-old widowed mother who'd begun dating. He's been helping her write her online profile and vetting prospective suitors. It got him thinking about if he weren't happily married. He blurted out, "If I weren't married, I'd definitely want to date you." Sweet man. Of course, when one is married, it is very safe to spew such sentiments. Toward the end of the conversation, he said he thought I was "smokin' hot," which made this overweight, crow's feet-festoon 55-year-old feel very nice indeed.

Several friends have long-term marriages with younger men. I could see how it could work if the couples were compatible. After all, in the grand scheme, does age really matter? He could have health challenges before she does. And since women's life span is longer, she'd be able to have a sweetheart into her elder years.

Most of us don't like to think long term. We want to enjoy the magic of now and believe we'll figure out what we need when the time comes. So why not embrace the situation if a there's a mutual attraction with a younger man and see where it goes?

As long as you both are clear that you want similar things out of life, then an age difference doesn't really matter. However, my experience is that a man a decade or so younger typically has children at home, or is consumed by his career, or doesn't really have time or the means to travel or accompany me in the life I've created. If so, great. But I've found it's rare.

So should you throw caution to the wind and play with your boy toy? Or is that disrespectful to him, implying that you will discard him when he's no longer fun to play with? But isn't that a possibility no matter what his age? And, of course he could jettison you just as easily.

What's your philosophy about midlife women dating a man over a decade younger? Have you done it? What did you learn?

Falling for potential

When we are younger, with our lives yet to be determined, we can fall in love with someone's potential, not who they are at the moment. I know I have.

A pal wrote today, "I have fallen in love more times than I care to count with the highest potential of a woman, rather than with the woman herself, and I have hung on to the relationship for a long time (sometimes far too long) waiting for the woman to ascend to her own greatness. Many times in romance I have been a victim of my own optimism."

Which makes me wonder: Are we just seeing them as we think they can be? Or are we projecting our desires onto them when they have no inclination to become what we see?

When we see them as "bigger" (more successful, fulfilling a future we see they can have), are we tapping into the best we see for them? This can be empowering ("I believe in you, baby," "I know you can do it") or demeaning ("I know you didn't do your best," "If you only did what I suggested you'd be more successful").

But if our beloved doesn't share our vision for him

and has no desire for what we think is possible for him, both become unhappy. You are constantly disappointed by his lack of progress toward what you see as his greatness, and he feels a constant environment of disapproval and failure.

At this point in our lives, most of us have achieved something — yet not all that we imagined for ourselves. So seeing your sweetheart's potential can be a marvelous gift to someone who may feel they are treading water toward retirement but had hoped to accomplish more. They've just become burnt out at how hard it has been to accomplish what they desired. Some people have abandoned their dreams and a cheerleader may be just what they need.

However, if your snookems is content to glide by at their current state and not aspire to more, your prodding him to reach his potential will be irksome.

When starting to date someone, I think it's important within the first few months to discuss each of your visions for the future as well as dreams. If you are an achiever who believes in constantly improving and striving, you're probably not going to be happy with someone who sees no need to change the status quo.

It can be sad to realize you see someone's greater potential and your sweetie doesn't see himself similarly. But if this is important to you, best to move on as otherwise you'll be doomed for decades of disappointment.

I guess it shouldn't be "love is blind" but perhaps "love sees the other as they may never see themselves."

"He likes to wear the pants in the relationship"

A good pal was telling me about a middle-aged, tall, athletic, single lawyer friend of his. I said, "He sounds like someone I'd like."

My friend responded, "I don't think it would be a good match. He likes to wear the pants in the relationship."

I was taken aback.

Responding as non-defensively as I could muster, I said, "I like a man to wear the pants, too. I'm not interested in a subordinate or timid man. I want an equal partner, not someone who dominates nor subordinates himself."

I wondered if this was a common assumption strong women face. Their friends think because they are assertive, accomplished and ambitious, she wants to dominate the relationship. I know some women do. But not all.

No wonder it can be difficult for powerful women to be set up by their friends. If their pals think they only want submissive men and the friends only know powerful men, they won't think the two could be a match. How sad.

I know I assume that my friends know me well enough to know I don't have to always be the alpha. But clearly that isn't the case. So what's a formidable gal to do?

It seems a frank conversation is called for, explaining to one's friends what you are looking for. Not only the superficial trappings (has a job, good dresser, well groomed, smart, mannerly, at least 6′ tall), but the personality traits as well. It's always good to describe the values you want to share, although friends may have no idea if someone is a cheater, closet alcoholic, or privately verbally abusive.

Have you experienced your friends assuming you'd like — or not like — a certain type of man and they are wrong? How'd you set them straight?

Finding happiness

At a recent closing conference luncheon, the next host country, China, provided beautiful scrolls with a different saying on each. There was no notation on the beautiful red box which saying was inside.

Several at my table unfurled theirs to have our Chinese table host read the calligraphy. "Happiness" read a few. "Long life" said the others, including mine. Thinking for a moment, I decided I didn't want long life unless happiness accompanied it. I didn't want to be miserable in old age.

So I unrolled the extra scroll at our table and hopefully held it for our host to read. "Long life" she announced. Drat!

I was determined, so I went to an empty table and began untying scrolls. I'd now learned how to tell the difference between the two messages. One after another read "long life." I could have stopped, but I was searching for happiness!

I carefully retied each scroll as I continued my search. After a dozen or so, finally, happiness was found! How does this apply to dating — and life?

I was clear on what I wanted and unwilling to compromise. I could have just walked away with long life and taken a philosophical stance that one makes one's own happiness, no matter what. Sure. Sounds good.

But since I knew I wanted happiness and it was out there, I just needed to put a little effort into finding it. With a little diligence, I found it.

In dating, you can settle for less than you really want and convince yourself you will make it work. Or you can say, "I know what I want and am willing to keep searching until I find it."

I will now hang both scrolls in my home as a reminder that I can have both, with clarity and persistence.

And I hope my future partner realizes that I searched hard to find him to enjoy long life and happiness with him.

Resources

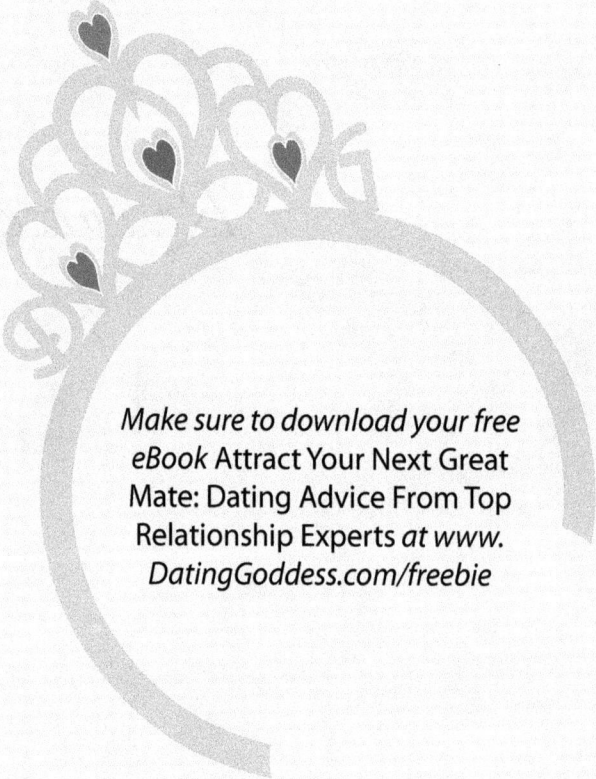

Make sure to download your free eBook Attract Your Next Great Mate: Dating Advice From Top Relationship Experts at www. DatingGoddess.com/freebie

Afterword

At the time of this writing, I have not yet found my true King Charming. I continue my search with verve. I've become more discerning about what I want and don't want. I've met some wonderful men pals — my treasures — who continue to be in touch.

I wish you much luck in your adventure. It will be fun and frustrating, exhilarating and exasperating, and sexy or sexless. So much depends on you, your approach and your attitude. My books are designed to help you enjoy as much as possible and ward off unpleasantness. But nearly all adventures have wonderful highs as well as a few lows. If you know that going in and arm yourself with information on what to expect, you'll have more of the positives and fewer of the negatives.

Please drop by www.DatingGoddess.com and join in the discussion and report on your experiences.

Dating Goddess

Resources

o to www.datinggoddess.com to access a variety of useful resources. We work to suggest resources we think have value.

Dating and relationship book reviews

These reviews will save you time and money as I've given you my take on specific books, CDs and more. Some are worth your effort to buy and read or listen to them — some are not. We're always adding new book reviews, so check frequently. We'll also notify our mailing list when new resources are added.

Dating site links

There are a lot of dating sites on the Internet. I've listed the ones I think are worth investigating.

Dating products and tools

Dating can be daunting. We're continually looking at

ways to make it easier and more fun. We'll provide info on games, tools, even date-wear that will help others know you're available, or help you get to know potential suitors better.

Dating and relationship advice sites

Advice "experts" abound on the Internet as anyone can self-proclaim themseves as expert — even if they haven't dated in 30 years and never in midlife. I've worked to find experts who's advice I generally think is solid.

Midlife recources

We'll feature Web sites, books, events and other resources we think might interest you.

Newly discovered resources

I'll add other resources as we discover them, subscribe to our mailing list to get the scoop as soon as we find them. Go to www.DatingGoddess.com to register for our mailing list. Don't worry, we won't sell or give your email to anyone.

Acknowledgments

Let me start by acknowledging the 112 men who helped trigger the lessons contained in this book. Some prompted several! They remain nameless here to protect their identity, although most would recognize references to them. Plus the thousands more whose winks, emails and calls didn't result in a date, but helped me learn the dating game. And all those men who I emailed who never responded — such a blessing to have them weed themselves out.

> I acknowledge the 112 men who triggered my lessons

I'd like to thank my Seven Sisters mastermind group for the tremendous brainstorming, noodling, strategizing and encouragement. I wouldn't have begun this project without the prodding of Val Cade, Chris Clarke-Epstein, Mariah Burton Nelson, Sue Dyer, Sam Horn and Marilynn Mobley.

Thank you to my good friends who've listened to my dating stories ad nauseam, and whose support and wisdom are embedded in this text. Ed Betts, Ken Braly, Bruce Daley, Tom Drews, Elaine Floyd, Paulette Ensign, Scott Friedman, Craig Harrison, Mary Jansen, Tom Johnson, Sandy Jones, Mary Kilkenny, Ellie Klevins, Patrick Lynch, Mary Marcdante, Barbara McNichol, Ann Peterson, Anthony Ramsey, Caterina Rando, Kristy Rogers, Jana Stanfield, Holly Steil, Terry Tepliz, and George Walther, thank you.

The Adventures in Delicious Dating After 40 series

The Adventures in Delicious Dating After 40 series is designed to help you understand your own midlife dating journey. It is not a road map, as we all take different routes. It is a guide to help you understand yourself, midlife men, and the dating process. Hopefully, you'll not only learn from the lessons and insights shared in this series, but you'll examine how they apply — or don't — to your own dating adventure.

You'll get the scoop on what you need to know, what's changed since you last dated, and how to navigate inevitable bumps in the road.

Following is an overview of each book in the series and a sampling of some of the chapter titles. All are detailed at www.DatingGoddess.com.

Date or Wait: Are You Ready for Mr. Great?

Are you ready for a special man in your life? You have a great life. But you know you'd like a special man to share it. You think you're ready to date, but you haven't done it in a while.

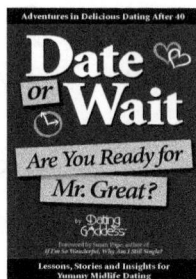

What should you consider before you actually start dating full bore? Even if you've reentered the dating world, this will give you a foundation of attitude and philosophy to make your adventure more fulfilling.

Sample chapters

From hurt to flirt

Dating is like Baskin-Robbins

You've got to kiss a lot of…princes!

What's your definition of dating success?

Are you open to receiving?

Dating: A self-designed personal-growth workshop

Hands-on dating research

Being present to the presents

Being aggressively single

Approaching dating like a buffet

Is Brad Pitt ruining your love life?

Treasures can come in dented packages

Assessing Your Assets: Why You're A Great Catch

You have many wonderful qualities. But it's easy to focus on one's flaws — at least what seem like flaws to you. However, to the right man your imperfections are endearing, attractive and lovable. You have to be clear what you offer a man who will find you enchanting.

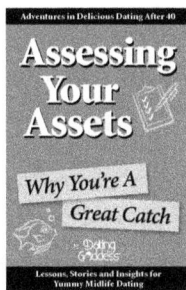

Assessing Your Assets helps you look at what you bring to a new relationship. It will help you see your good points so you'll approach dating with more confidence.

Sample chapters

💜 Don't think you are damaged goods

💜 You are (probably) more attractive than you think!

💜 They aren't called "hate handles"

💜 Are you a good man picker?

💜 What are your deal breakers?

💜 Are you arguing your limitations?

💜 Turn your liabilities into assets

💜 The strong vs. nice woman debate

💜 Is your sense of humor stunting your dating?

💜 Why are we drawn to bad boys?

💜 The zest test

In Search of King Charming: Who Do I Want to Share My Throne?

You are no longer looking for "Prince" Charming because you are a queen. You want someone who is at your level, not groveling at your feet. You want a king — someone who's your equal and with whom you can rule the throne together!

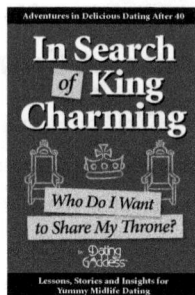

This book focuses on helping you better define what you want beyond tall, dark and handsome! You'll consider characteristics you might not have thought of before. You'll look at what you want now.

Sample chapters

💜 Building your Franken-boyfriend

💜 What's your "perfect boyfriend's" job description?

💜 A man to go with your wardrobe

💜 In search of the elusive good kisser

💜 When you're clear on what you want, it appears

💜 Are you dating the same guy in different bodies?

💜 Does he fit in your world?

💜 What's your kissing quotient?

💜 Is your guy's loving muscle strong?

💜 Do you both have the same dating rhythm?

Embracing Midlife Men: Insights Into Curious Behaviors

Do you sometimes scratch your head after interacting with a midlife man, wondering, "What could he possibly be thinking?" Especially if it's before, during or after a date with a man who presumably wants to impress you!

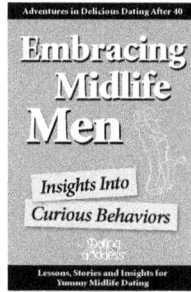

This book focuses on better understanding midlife men's behaviors. When you grasp what's going on in his head it's much easier to embrace him. Men are wondrous creatures, so we need to understand them better and love them for who they are.

Sample chapters

💜 Men are like shoes

💜 Why men disappear when it gets serious

💜 Chivalry isn't dead —but it seems to be hibernating

💜 Do men want feisty women?

💜 Midlife men have forgotten how to date

💜 Are you getting prime time from your man?

💜 When a man tells you what he paid for things

💜 Does he treat you like his ex?

💜 Has Greg Behrendt done women a disservice?

💜 Tales of woo

Dipping Your Toe in the Dating Pool: Dive In Without Belly Flopping

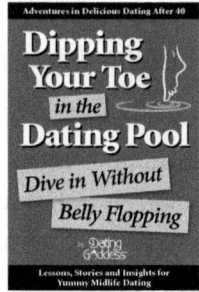

You've decided you are ready — you want to start dating. Maybe you've already had a few coffee dates with several men. You want to be as successful as possible on your dating adventure.

This book focuses on getting started on your dating adventures. We cover what you need to know as you begin your journey.

♥ Do you have the right datewear?

♥ Dating with integrity

♥ Building your rejection muscle

♥ When "be yourself" is questionable advice

♥ Faux beaus and practice dating

♥ Are you making bad decisions out of loneliness?

♥ Being "in wonder" about your date's behavior

♥ When do you feel most vulnerable in dating?

♥ Are you out of his league — or he yours?

♥ Why listening is so seductive

Winning at the Online Dating Game: Stack the Deck in Your Favor

Internet dating can be frustrating or fruitful. It will be much less exasperating if you know how to read and weed out men's profiles that aren't appropriate for you. And you'll have a steady stream of potential suitors if you know how to write a compelling profile for yourself.

This book focuses on the ins and outs of online dating. How to play the game, which has it's own rules and language. If you don't understand how online dating works, you'll waste a lot of time connecting with men who are not a possible fit for you.

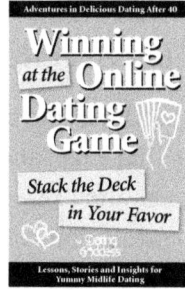

Sample chapters

- Shopping for men
- Safe online dating
- Is 21st Century dating unnatural?
- What do men look at in your profile?
- Euphemisms uncovered
- Are you describing yourself compellingly?
- No, I will not be dating your Harley
- Playing the online dating game
- Scantily clothed pictures

Check Him Out Before Going Out: Avoiding Dud Dates

Adventures in Delicious Dating After 40

Check Him Out *Before* **Going Out**

Avoiding Dud Dates

Dating Goddess

Lessons, Stories and Insights for Yummy Midlife Dating

Under the cloak of the anonymity that email and the phone provides, men often reveal more than they intend. If you ask the right questions you can find out a lot about his values and view of the world after just an interaction or two.

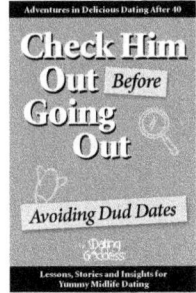

This book focuses on what you need to ask before agreeing to even a coffee date. You need to vet the men who email and call you to ensure you're not likely to waste your time with men who clearly aren't a match.

Sample chapters

❤ Becoming smitten with the fantasy

❤ Can Google help — or hinder — your dating life?

❤ Qualify your potential dates before meeting

❤ The art of consideration

❤ Anticipating a big date is like awaiting Santa

❤ Being seduced by what he is over who he is

❤ Are you his spare?

❤ My boyfriend, whom I haven't met

❤ When canceling is the right thing to do

❤ Politics, religion and sex — oh my!

First-Rate First Dates: Increasing the Chances of a Second Date

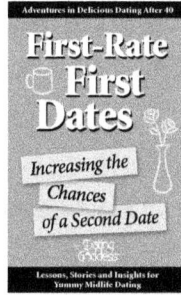

You can tell a lot about someone within the first 30 minutes. What does he talk about? Does he ask you questions? If so, what does he want to know about you? What do you need to know about him? How does he treat you? How does he treat those around you?

This book focuses on what goes on during the first date. How do you determine if you want a second date? What you can do to increase the likelihood your date will ask you for a second? That is if you want a repeat!

Sample chapters

💚 Start with coffee

💚 How do you greet him?

💚 When it clicks, throw out some of your criteria

💚 Tracking your date's score

💚 Clues a guy is just looking for a booty call

💚 12 signs he won't be asking for a second date

💚 First-date red flags that this guy isn't for you

💚 Honesty is not always the best policy

💚 Chemistry, or does he make my toes curl?

💚 Women's first-date blunders

Real Deal or Faux Beau: Should You Keep Seeing Him?

You've begun to go out with a man you like. How do you decide if you should continue seeing him, or if you should release him because he's not The One?

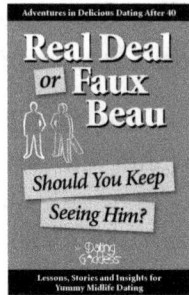

This book focuses on second dates and beyond. During the dating process you are both assessing if you want to keep seeing each other. This book helps you determine what questions you need to ask yourself.

Sample chapters

💜 Deciding to see him again or not

💜 What's your date's Delight/Disappointment Scale score?

💜 Broaching tough conversations

💜 "I want to respect me in the morning"

💜 Does he invite you to his place?

💜 Are you stingy in dating?

💜 When his hand is on your knee too soon

💜 Easy way to ask hard questions

💜 Rose-colored glasses obscure red flags

💜 If his stories don't add up, subtract yourself

Multidating Responsibly: Play the Field Without Being A Player

Playing the field is frowned on in some circles. There are definitely appropriate and inappropriate ways to date several men simultaneously.

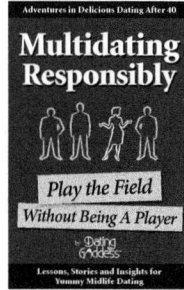

This book focuses on how to date around responsibly and with integrity without leading men on. If you do it with honesty, you can date several people at once until you're both ready to focus only on each other.

Sample chapters

💜 "Pimpin'" — Dating multiple guys

💜 Multi-dating pros and cons

💜 Your Date-A-Base — tracking multiple suitors

💜 "Hot bunking" your beaus

💜 Are you a "Let's Make a Deal" type of dater?

💜 Assume there are other women

💜 Dating's revolving door

💜 How long do you hedge your bet?

💜 Beware of multi-tasking when multi-dating

💜 Back burner beaus

💜 The boyfriend phone

Moving On Gracefully: Break Up Without Heartache

"Breaking up" sounds so high school, doesn't it? But part of the dating process is saying something when one of you decides not to date the other anymore. Going "poof" is not a mature or respectful option in midlife.

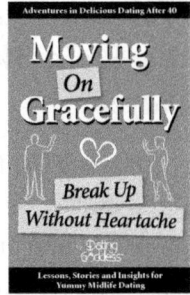

This book focuses on surviving a breakup, whether you initiate it or not. Either way, it's never easy to break up if you have developed any fondness toward the other.

Sample chapters

💚 Hello — goodbye: How to say no thanks after meeting

💚 Releasing back into the dating pool

💚 50 ways to leave your lover? 4 ways not to leave your suitor

💚 Breaking up is hard to do — right

💚 Why men go "poof"

💚 How to trump being dumped

💚 When breaking up is a "Get Out of Jail Free" card

💚 How to detect the end is near

💚 Failed relationships' blessings

💚 He's broken up with you — he just didn't tell you

💚 Rejection is protection

218

From Fear to Frolic: Get Naked Without Getting Embarrassed

This book focuses on what you need to consider and know before getting physically intimate with a man you're dating. This is nerve-wracking to many midlife women. This book will prepare you.

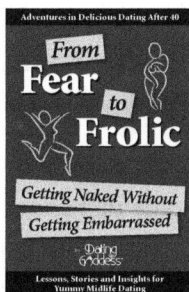

Sample chapters

💜 Sleepover do's and don'ts

💜 Does he want in your life — or just in your bedroom?

💜 Getting naked with him the first time

💜 An excuse to seduce or how important is bedroom bliss?

💜 What to ask yourself before getting naked with him

💜 Are you and your guy on the same sexual time line?

💜 Sharing your sexual owner's manual with him

💜 What women need from a man before having sex

💜 Why too-soon midlife sex is like non-fat food

💜 How dating sex is like waffles

💜 Too-soon seduction: "I'm special, but not THAT special"

Ironing Out Dating Wrinkles: Work Through Challenges Without Getting Steamed

Nearly all relationships have some ups and downs. Part of getting to know someone is knowing how they work through relationship misunderstandings.

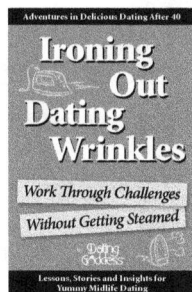

This book focuses on how to work through the inevitable hiccups that happen when you are getting to know each other. If you can both deal with challenges, the bond deepens and you find yourself smitten.

Sample chapters

❤ When your guy vexes you, ask what your highest self would do

❤ The first fight

❤ You want boo; he wants boo-ty

❤ Where's the line between getting your needs met and being selfish?

❤ Expressing your upset with your guy

❤ Is his toothbrush in your cabinet too soon?

❤ Do you love how he loves you?

❤ Is he collecting data on how to make you happy?

❤ Be careful of being smitten

❤ Exclusivity: How and when to broach it